GW00676515

THE
UNINTENTIONAL
MEDIUM

THE
UNINTENTIONAL
MEDIUM

BY SUZI SAMUEL

GOKO Management and Publishing
PO Box 7109
McMahons Point 2060
Sydney. Australia
Copyright © 2016 Suzi Samuel
All rights reserved.

In accordance with the U.S. Copyright Act of 1976, and the Australian Copyright Act of 1968 the scanning, uploading, and electronic sharing of any part of this book without the permission of the publisher constitutes unlawful piracy and theft of the author's intellectual property. If you would like to use material from the book (other than for review purposes), prior written permission must be obtained by contacting the publisher at info@Goko.com.au.

Library of Congress Cataloging-in-Publication Data
Samuel, Suzi
    The Unintentional Medium
        p. cm.

        ISBN: 978-1613397657
        LCCN: 2016933298

Book designed by DeeDee Heathman
Printed in Australia

For
David, the love of my life
And
Luisa, the light of my life

And in loving memory of
Stephen Speed and Annie Pelligrini

ACKNOWLEDGEMENTS

My special thanks to all those involved in the publication of "The Unintentional Medium."

To DeeDee Heathman, Kathy Knox, my super editor Kyra and especially the lovely Katherine Owen who really didn't want me to thank her publicly!

I would like to thank the lovely friends who have encouraged me in this adventure, jollied me along and provided glasses of champagne when needed.

To my gorgeous daughter Lulu and my wonderful husband David who has been a tower of strength and support. I couldn't have done it without you darling.

And last, but certainly not least, to Gran, Prucel, Mrs B and all those in the spirit world who have certainly made their presence felt in writing this book.

PROLOGUE

I stared at the pan of porridge. It glared back at me morosely, refusing to thicken properly and emitting the occasional gloop of a primordial swamp. I prodded it gingerly with my wooden spoon, half expecting something Jurassic to emerge from the murky depths.

"Must be Australian oats," I muttered darkly to myself. Having just moved Down Under, I was quick to blame any culinary mishap on "different ingredients".

I had just decided to try and beat the recalcitrant cereal into submission when a voice behind me said, "Just give it a gentle stir and a bit more time, dear. It will thicken up nicely. The oats need to absorb some more liquid."

It was my husband's grandmother, Prucel, a delightful, sprightly little lady who was ready to give me cooking tips, and to cheer me up when the occasional bout of homesickness hit, or when I felt lost and bewildered in my new country.

I turned back to the stove. Sure enough, after a couple of minutes of gentle stirring, my mess of porridge had transformed itself into an unctuous bowl of oatmeal.

"Thanks, Prucel."

"You are very welcome, dear," she replied as her smoky outline faded gently away, back into the spirit world.

This other world is now so much a part of my life that I no longer find it strange to be given cooking tips by someone who has been dead for forty years, but it wasn't always so. I'm not one of those mediums who have been seeing the departed from babyhood, and I have absolutely no recollection of benign shades peering into my cot. In fact, it was quite a shock when I first realised there was a parallel universe. Remember that fantastic Whoopi Goldberg moment in the film *Ghost* when she realised she was actually picking up a presence? Well, I can identify with that!

But back to the beginning.

CHAPTER 1

Sex, drugs, and rock 'n roll! The pill, pot, and the Rolling Stones! If you remember the sixties, you weren't really there.

My trouble is that I remember it only too well. I remember exactly where I was when Kennedy was shot, and a world that was shaken to its core by the events that took place that day in Dallas. I remember battling with the unrelenting winter of 1963 when we froze in homes without the comfort of central heating. I remember being too vain to wear sensible boots and somehow managing to walk on packed ice, using my stiletto heels like pitons. I remember the Beatles and the Rolling Stones, and I remember the mind-numbing boredom of growing up in the genteel environs of suburban London.

Apart from a few innocent fumblings in darkened cinemas, sex and drugs were non- existent, and rock 'n roll was confined to my Dansette record player. Not for us - the joys of the King's Road. We lived vicariously through eponymous tales of Mars bars in odd orifices, and free love fuelled by copious amounts of grass. Highly educated but totally naïve, we put the world to rights by debating existentialism and railing against the ordered confines of our conservative backgrounds. The nearest we got to rebellion was smoking French cigarettes and buying Bob Dylan hats.

Nevertheless, the pull of our upbringing was strong, and sooner rather than later, we settled into wedlock and conformity. Having survived a couple of painful and destructive relationships, I married my first husband, John, when I was twenty-two. He owned a very successful chain of South London betting shops, and I jumped eagerly from a dysfunctional life with my parents into the affluent arms of matrimony and a completely different world.

When I look back over all the houses I have lived in, it seems that all of them had some sort of presence lurking. The house I lived in until I was eleven always seemed a bit spooky. It was a typical Victorian semi, and the loo and bathroom were on the first floor. As a child, I was a real pain in the derrière because I would never venture to the loo unaccompanied after dark and usually made some poor soul stand guard. No-one was happy to leave the warm fire to sit in the sub-Polar regions of the stairs in the days before central heating.

I have no idea why I was so afraid, or what I thought would get me while I was ensconced. Perhaps it was something to do with the shadow of the hanged man on the next landing that could be seen at dusk. It was amazingly clear. You could see the rope and the outline of a man, head bent over, and he seemed to be wearing a long coat or dressing gown. Every time I mentioned it, one of the adults would say "Don't be silly, dear," or "It's just a trick of the light," or even, on one memorable occasion, "Please don't give that child cheese just before bed again." However, long after I too had joined the ranks of the grown-ups, I remember hearing vague mutterings about the old man who had committed suicide there at the end of the 19th century, before my grandparents moved in.

When I was twelve, we moved to a 1930's semi. From the minute I went into the house, I felt cold and uncomfortable. However, the atmosphere was lightened by the fact that the vendors had a Siamese cat which I cuddled, and which left more or less permanent cat hairs in my dark green school blazer.

In those days, a child certainly didn't have any input into the choice of abode, and anyway, my mother really liked the house. It was a dark house. It had dark wood paneling, dark wood parquet floors, and leaded windows that didn't let in much light. There was one bedroom that scared the living daylights out of me. Every time I went in there I would start to shiver and the hair would stand up on the nape of my neck. It was certainly a good few degrees colder than the rest of the house. My parents tried to say that it was because the room was over a garage, but as that house didn't have central heating either and was as cold as charity anyway, I don't know if it made much difference. All I know is there was something intrinsically evil in that room, and years later, when my daughter went to stay with Grannie and Gramps, I made sure she stayed well away from it.

My mother went back to work when I was eleven, something quite unusual in those days, so when I got back from school at about 4.30p.m. I had the house to myself for a couple of hours. In some respects, this wasn't a bad thing because, being a studious little bunny, I could get on with my homework. However, going into the empty house, especially in the winter when it was dark, was not pleasant and I think it was against my father's religion to leave on a light. For some obscure reason, the light switch was in the middle of the hall, and so when I got home, I would open the front door, peer suspiciously around, leap for the light switch, scuttle back to close the front door and then hightail it into the kitchen where I would hole up until Mummy or Daddy got home!

It was, therefore, a great relief when I got married and moved into a brand new flat in the posh, leafy suburb of Wimbledon, where things were relatively peaceful on the spiritual front and seemed to continue that way in our next home, a town house in a cul-de-sac. We moved to this mini Knots Landing where women forged lasting friendships in kitchens over endless coffee and cigarettes. Two years later, our beautiful daughter, Luisa, was born. We travelled extensively and eventually bought an apartment in Villefranche Sur Mer on the French Riviera.

However, when I was twenty-nine, my first husband, John, collapsed very suddenly with kidney failure and spent his remaining five years on dialysis or, for some of the time, with a transplanted kidney. This was in the early seventies when organ transplants were at quite an embryonic stage, and our lives lurched from crisis to crisis. My daughter, Lulu, was three when her daddy got sick, and trying to juggle hospitals with keeping life as normal as possible for my little girl was at times a little difficult.

One of those still enduring friendships is with a very close friend called Sue. She is a tiny, elegant woman with an inexhaustible supply of energy and a great sense of fun and naughtiness. We have known each other for over thirty years, and in times of trouble, she has been a rock. When the children were small, we would spend many an hour in one kitchen or another, putting the world to rights or just generally gossiping, and she was a great comfort to me when I was in need. One day I was telling her about the latest traumas over one of our interminable cups of coffee and I said, "Sue, I really can't see an end to this and I can't see a way for things to improve."

Having clucked and hugged and provided Kleenex and more coffee, she said, "I know. Why don't you go and see a clairvoyant?"

"A what?" At this stage I didn't even know my star sign and had no idea there was a whole other world out there.

"A clairvoyant."

"But I've never been to one. Have you?"

"No, but I'll come with you and hold your hand."

"Are you going to see her too?"

"No fear!"

Anyway, one glorious afternoon a couple of days later, off we went to see a lady called Mary West. We parked in front of a neat semi-detached house with frilly lace curtains at the windows and a riot of daffodils in the front garden. Fearfully, knees knocking like castanets, we rang the bell and waited, expecting at the very least Madame Arcati and ectoplasm. However, we were greeted by a cuddly blonde lady of indeterminate age, festooned in pink frills. We sat down for a cup of tea and a cosy chat surrounded by poodles – real, stuffed, and China, and one I wasn't quite sure was real, stuffed, or maybe both!

All she knew about me was my name and, as I was only thirty-two at the time, it seemed very unlikely I was about to become a widow.

She took my hands in hers. "What sad little hands. Don't worry, dear. In two years' time you will have everything you ever wanted. You will have happiness, riches, and a very successful man who adores you but who is much older than you."

When I quizzed her on the immediate future, all she would say was, "You have a rocky road ahead of you. Make sure your child is secure."

A year later, in 1980, John, and my beloved grandmother died.

Hindsight is a wonderful thing and, knowing what I now know about the spirit world, I do believe there could have been some malevolent presence lurking in our seemingly peaceful neighbourhood. Ours was not the only tragedy. The people who bought our house went very unexpectedly bankrupt. My friend's son was tragically killed just after his eighteenth birthday. Another friend's husband was killed when she was two months pregnant, and there were other unexpected and unexplained deaths and divorces, quite out of proportion to the size of the community.

The long arm of whatever lurked in the Close didn't let go easily. One of my dearest friends is a super lady called Birgit, who is very precious to me. She and her divine husband, Bob, went back home to live in the States, and Birgit then had to undergo a hysterectomy. It should have been a comparatively simple routine procedure, but something went wrong and she spent six weeks on life support. Thank God she somehow came through it and is now fine, but it was touch and go at the time.

Two of the residents who were not quite so lucky were a South African couple called Elbie and Johann. He was a lawyer working for the South African government, and suburban myth had it that he was a spy. I'm sure it can't have been true, but at the time it was a good story, especially as he used to go mountaineering, supposedly, out of reach for days at a time.

When they were posted home to SA, Johann resigned his job and went to work as a lawyer in a tiny Transvaal town. One day, out of nowhere, a car screeched through the sleepy main street, squashed Johann dead, and left in a cloud of dust, never to be seen again.

A few months later, a handsome young stranger arrived in town. Now, Elbie was a darling, but not the prettiest of women, and not really the type to inspire flaming passion in a young man's breast, but this seemed to be the case and the young Adonis wooed Elbie ardently. Elbie succumbed and, having arranged a sleepover for her daughter, spent the night with the young man. At some time during the night, she died of an apparent asthma attack. The young man disappeared without a trace.

Now, in the midst of all this drama and tragedy, there was one small incident I recall. Until John went into the hospital, we had never spent a night apart. At weekends, Lulu used to go to my parents so I could spend the weekend at the hospital. It was quite tiring rushing to the hospital and trying to ensure Lulu's life was as normal as possible and so, by the time I got home at about 10p.m. on a Saturday night, I was bushed. My treat was getting into bed with a tuna and chopped onion sandwich (something you can only do on your own) to watch TV knowing I could sleep undisturbed without having to listen out for a small child.

At that particular time, *Starsky and Hutch* was on the television and I loved watching that. One episode was particularly scary, about a man who thought he was a vampire. Now, I don't do vampires and have never been able to watch a Dracula movie. When the programme finished, I turned out the light and pulled the duvet firmly over my head so that if the Count did sniff me out in deepest Wimbledon, he wouldn't be able to see me!

In the middle of the night something woke me. At first, having been deeply asleep, I couldn't make out where I was or why I was on my own, but as I gradually started to come to, I looked around the room. There, in the entrance to the bathroom, was what looked like a huge bat! Petrified, I leapt out of bed and rushed onto the landing where my Bassett Hound was happily snoring in his basket.

"Wake up!" I yelled, kicking the basket. I grabbed the poor dog by the collar and dragged him into the bedroom. Still keeping a tight hold of him, with trembling fingers I turned on the light to see … a jacket on a coat hanger that I had hung on the bathroom door! I must say, I felt a complete idiot and was glad I had only Barnaby Bassett to witness the scene. He was astounded and happy because I actually invited him to sleep on the bed with me instead of giving him the usual clout when I found him snuggled up in the duvet.

About eighteen months after John's death, I went to a drinks party given by my lovely American neighbours. We were a small, very sociable community and got together regularly. One of this group was a charming, urbane man called Laurie who was the director of an international clearing bank. He lived a few doors down the road from me and had sadly lost his wife to cancer a couple of years before. On this particular occasion, fuelled by sunshine and champagne, he made a beeline for me and invited me to dinner that evening. We dined at the Mayfair Hilton, still quite posh in those days, and after dinner we went for a walk in one of the most romantic spots in London, St James' Park. We stood on the little bridge over the lake and watched the moonlight reflected in the water.

After that evening, we soon became inseparable, in spite of the twenty-five-year age gap, much to the delight of everyone except his three daughters who were almost the same age as me. When Laurie talked about marrying me, I was adamant he sort out his will, leaving everything to his daughters. I had been left comfortably off and didn't need his money. Even this didn't convince The Three Graces I wasn't a gold digger, and they lost no opportunity to point out the age difference to their father and imply that the world and his wife were sniggering at him behind his back.

In spite of this we continued dating and then, just before Christmas, we decided to go for a short break in the Cotswolds. Laurie shied away from the idea of taking me to the posh hotel he'd stayed in before in case someone recognised him, so he booked to take his "bit of fluff" to another hotel.

The hotel turned out to be a charming old manor house with a wonderful collection of Russell Flint paintings. We were shown up to our room, which was delightfully English; all exposed beams and chintz.

It had obviously been fitted out in more trusting days because the old wooden door didn't have a lock, just a latch.

We went to dinner, which was excellent, and only slightly marred by the guilty look on Laurie's face and the furtive glances he kept casting round the dining room, as if he expected Pinkerton's Detective Agency to catch up with him at any moment. Having got through the meal without attracting too much attention, in spite of Laurie's demeanour, we went up to bed.

Now at this point, even though I had been on the receiving end of old Mary's predictions, I had absolutely no knowledge of the spirit world. At about 2.30a.m. something awoke me. There was a dim light from a street lamp coming through the curtains and I lay there thinking what a delightful hotel it was. I looked towards the door. As I watched, transfixed, what looked like a hand with five elongated smoky fingers reached through the door and made as if to open the latch. I let out a piercing scream. Laurie shot bolt upright in bed, clutching his heart.

"What's going on? What's the matter?"

I was still screaming. "It's a ghost! Do something!"

By this time the whole hotel must have been awake. Laurie turned on the light and stuffed an angina pill. "There's nothing there. You must have imagined it."

I shouldn't think there was anything there anymore. I had probably frightened the poor ghost to death.

We got some strange looks at breakfast that morning. I'm sure at least a couple of the other guests thought Laurie was a girlfriend beater!

At that time, my mother worked for an English Lord who had a country estate very near the hotel. I didn't tell her about the spectral visitation, but I did mention that I'd stayed there.

"It's a lovely hotel," said Mummy, "but it's very haunted."

"What do you mean?"

"Well, the butler told me there is a grey lady who is often seen walking the corridors."

Now she tells me!

Anyway, as the predictions had been so accurate, I decided to go back to old Mary and the poodles, eager to know the fairytale future ahead of me. Well! What a difference!

"It will end in tears," she said. "He is leading you up the garden path and will drop you at the back gate." I couldn't believe my ears. Where was my happy ever after? This man was perfect for me and I thought we were idyllically happy. Nevertheless, she was right.

Meanwhile, several of my friends had been to see her. One, a beautiful, bright thirty-seven-year-old who seemed to be in a great relationship was told, "No happiness until you are forty-eight." Another was told, "Ten years of misery ahead." They all reeled out of there in shock, but everything she predicted happened.

After this, I was a little wary and tended to shy away from things supernatural.

During the eighties I had some very good friends called Marcelle and Pierre, who lived in the most charming doll's house near Harrods. Marcelle, a skilled beautician by trade, was the epitome of a chic French woman, albeit from a slightly earlier era. She had perfect olive skin and glossy black hair, always beautifully styled in a soigné French pleat, and from time to time was even known to sport a beret. She used to talk about "my little Pierre" and I expected him to be equally Gallic, but when I met him he was the archetypal English gentleman. He was called Peter Billingham, and he sported such a splendid ginger handlebar moustache that he made me think immediately of the gentleman with foxy whiskers in Jemima Puddleduck!

Marcelle was a fantastic cook with a motherly manner, and a motley crew of her "naufragés" – castaways – would gather around the table for evenings of fantastic food, fun, and vast quantities of wine.

She had a strong belief in the spirit world and was friendly with a medium from Weston-super-Mare called Mrs. Butterfield who she was, for some reason, eager for me to meet. Mrs. Butterfield was a very different kettle of fish from the doom and gloom of Mary. She was a sweet-faced, roly-poly country woman who had lived all her life in

Somerset. It says something for Marcelle's powers of persuasion that she made the trek to London, but thanks to a large dose of Gallic charm and the thought of a few days of wonderful food, she sallied forth. Worth I met her in Marcelle's kitchen, she eyed me knowingly. I almost had the sense that she thought things had fallen into place.

"Oh, yes. Here you are at last, my dear. I knew you'd come one day soon."

Mrs. B was a great source of strength and comfort to me during some rather turbulent years, and she sort of adopted me. During one visit she said to me, "One day, my dear, you will be doing what I'm doing," at which point I told her not to be such a silly old woman. However, Mrs. B was a very determined old lady. Not long after this chat she became ill and sadly died.

And my life altered completely.

CHAPTER 2

When Mrs. B died, I obviously wanted to pay my last (as I thought) respects, but I didn't much fancy the trek to Weston-super-Mare on my own, so I commandeered the company of Joy. Joy is my best friend, adopted big sister, and partner in crime. She was my next door neighbour in Knots Landing. I call her Joyous because she makes my life joyous. She always complains because, being slightly deaf, if I get her bad ear, she thinks I'm calling her Joyce, which she can't stand. Anyway, having asked, wheedled, blackmailed, and called in any outstanding favours I could think of, a reluctant Joy agreed to come with me.

On a miserably cold, dank November day, Joy and I got our suitably black fur coats out of mothballs and set off for Weston-super-Mare. We rolled down the M4 and the fog rolled in. We eventually got to Mrs. B's modest semi to find cars double parked on the road outside and the house heaving. We squeezed our way through the throng to find Mr. B.

"Hello. We are friends of Mrs. B from London. She was such a lovely lady and we are so sorry for your loss."

"Lunnen? Did you say Lunnen?"

"Yes, that's right."

Word spread around the house like an Australian bush fire. "They're from Lunnen. These folks have come all the way from Lunnen."

A path cleared before us like the parting of the Red Sea. The house became still, and with great ceremony and in reverent silence, we were ushered into the tiny hall where we were installed on two hardback chairs under the cage of a round butterball of a canary. There we sat in our fur coats, exuding the faint smell of naphthalene, like Patience on a monument, with the assembled company regarding us as some sort of alien beings. Having reduced the house to silence, we didn't think it appropriate to talk to each other, although I think I caught the faint whisper of "I'll get you for this," or "You owe me big time."

All this time there was no sign of the hearse and people started to twitch slightly. Eventually someone broke the silence (engendered by us) and asked Mr. B where the coffin was. In a wonderful West Country burr came the reply, "Oh, Doreen, she just done popped to Shepton Mallet!"

With coffin? Without coffin? Corporeally? Spiritually? It's one of those questions you don't want to ask because reality could be a dreadful disappointment.

Eventually the hearse arrived and we all piled into our cars and set off for the local Spiritualist Church. We rocketed off at a rate of knots. The hearse driver had obviously done rallying at some point and it was quite a challenge keeping up with him. An awful lot of right hand turns seemed to be involved in the journey and as we screeched around yet another corner on two wheels, Joy said, "For God's sake keep up and don't lose them. There are thirty cars following you!"

Having safely made it, convoy still intact, the service was lovely, although I did notice Joy had gone a bit pale and had a strange expression on her face. When the service was over, I discovered the reason. Now, Joy isn't a believer in the spirit world but is not averse to throwing out the odd challenge. She had been married to a doctor who beat her up so badly that some days her face would be unrecognisable, but then had the nerve to speak convincingly about the level of violence in casualty wards. During one onslaught he had perforated her eardrum which, at the time of the funeral, had been especially troublesome for a few weeks. She later told me that during the service, she had said, "Okay, Mrs. B. If you're so clever, do something about my ear." At which point her ear improved enormously, giving Joyous pause for thought!

Even before Mrs. Butterfield decided to pass on her mantle, I realised very early on in my newly single state that if, at a party or dinner, you listened very carefully to what people told you during the course of the evening, you could then tell them virtually the same things back whilst gazing into their eyes and pretending to read their hands. Let me tell you, men fell for it every time. It was one of my most successful ploys and I milked it for all it was worth.

One evening I was at a dinner party, sitting next to a very tasty film director called Roger. "Aha!" I thought to myself. "Wouldn't mind a bit of that!"

"Let me read your hand," I cooed sweetly, taking his hand in both of mine. My hosts, who knew me well, tittered into their napkins. I told him things I had picked up during the course of dinner. Roger's eyes narrowed quizzically. He has always been able to see through me, which is probably why we remained such great friends from that evening on.

"You got divorced when you were thirty-two," I continued.

His vivid blue eyes shot wide open. "How the devil did you know that?"

All scepticism had vanished.

I was taken aback. "You must have told me," I replied honestly.

"I certainly did not. I don't know where that came from." He glared at our hosts who had stopped giggling and were gazing at me in astonishment. "You must have told her." They shook their heads. I was actually quite shaken. How could I have known?

Anyway, the main thing was, it worked. Roger and I were together, on and off, for the next ten years, and he is Lulu's honorary godfather. When she was sixteen she went to do her A-Levels at his old school, Bryanston. Once he had gotten over the shock of girls being allowed into the hallowed halls, he was delighted and came down with me one day to take her out to lunch. One of my abiding memories was of Roger pacing up and down a courtyard until coming to a sudden stop. Lu and I looked on in amazement.

"This is exactly where my bed used to be," said Roger, beaming happily.

He directed a fantastic television series called *Auf Wiedersehen, Pet,* which was a great hit in the eighties. He needed to go on a location-finding trip to Spain and suggested Lulu and I went along. The week before we were due to leave, we had just finished dinner and I said, "The next dinner together will be next Tuesday in Spain."

He raised an eyebrow. "I don't know when you're going, darling, but I'm going on Wednesday!"

I had booked the wrong day!

In light of what happened, I'm sure the spirit world tipped my hand. Lulu and I had a great flight out on Tuesday and settled into our hotel, expecting Roger to join us the next day, the very day when the French air traffic controllers decided to go on strike. It took poor old Rog and the rest of the film crew about fifteen hours to get to Malaga, having had to land twice in Portugal and once in Gibraltar en route. This was in the days before mobile phones, but I had twigged what was going on.

Lulu and I went to dinner in the hotel. Suddenly, there was an almighty kerfuffle and a huge, dishevelled figure burst through the door. Lulu took one look at him and burst into noisy sobs.

"Whatever is the matter?" I asked, relieved to see Roger in whatever condition.

"He's been in a plane crash!" sobbed Lulu.

Sartorial elegance has never been Roger's strong point.

Not long after this, I started to say strange things and became aware of even stranger happenings. I was going to a tennis tournament at the Albert Hall with my friend Mike, and on the drive there he was complaining about his job.

"Don't worry, you will be offered a job in a tent or a box at a sporting occasion when the flowers are blooming."

"What did you just say?"

"God knows!"

"Christ, we're in for a good evening. You haven't even had a drink yet!"

Six months later we were at the Stella Artois Tournament at Queen's Club, and as we stood sipping champagne, surrounded by beautiful roses, Mike said, "Guess what? I'm being head-hunted. I'm having lunch with the MD in the marquee on Final's Day."

When they had picked me up out of the roses, dusted me off and replenished the champagne, Mike's girlfriend, Barbie, said, "I wonder if what you told me will happen."

"What the devil did I tell *you*?"

"You told me that I would get a new job starting on your birthday (24th October, which fell on a Tuesday that year) for a salary two-thirds more than I'm getting at the moment."

Well, guess what, folks? It happened!

A few weeks later, Barbie called me. "What are you doing tomorrow evening?"

"Nothing," I replied, thinking, "Goody, dinner," because she is an excellent cook.

"I've booked you a client for a reading."

"Argh!"

Forget driving tests, A-levels, and final exams - this was one of the scariest moments of my life, which actually became even scarier when I realised I had picked up so much about this complete stranger's background. I had really been thrown in at the deep end. It was one of the most difficult readings I have ever done because the poor lady had suffered dreadful abuse as a child. It almost made me give up my psychic career before it had got started, but then Pat and little Alun who ran the local greengrocers sent me my second client. He was a very small man from the India/Pakistan border region and, unfortunately, he thought he had an appointment with a hooker!

I didn't realise this at first. I sat him down at the breakfast room table with a cup of tea. I thought he looked a bit surprised, but I carried on regardless. I took his hands in mine. He leered and stroked my palms. I started to realise something was amiss. Once a teacher, always a teacher, and anyway, he was smaller than me.

"Behave yourself!" I boomed in my best school marm voice. "Do you want this reading or not?"

The poor man was quite taken aback. "Er, yes" he stuttered, looking more bewildered by the minute.

I grasped his now sweaty palms and carried on with the reading. Now, this one too proved difficult because he had lost family during Partition, and my mind was filled with images of death and destruction. He did, nevertheless, thank me at the end of the session, though I'm not sure if his heart was in it. He certainly hadn't got what he came for!

Around this time, strange events started to occur. By now Lulu was about thirteen and just at the age when she and her friends would lock themselves in her room and discuss things that are all-encompassing for teenage girls. Mummy was definitely not cool and any trace of concern as to her adolescent well-being was met with withering looks and/or grunts.

One day I was in the kitchen when I heard what sounded like a buffalo stampede accompanied by shrieks and cries of, "Mummy!", "Sue!"

I rushed out to be almost skittled by Lulu, Gaby, and Alex hurtling down the stairs and then clinging to me for dear life.

"What on earth's the matter?"

"Ttttere's ssssomething on the sssstairs!"

God, can you get LSD at thirteen in Wimbledon Village? "What sort of something?"

"I don't know – a something outside your bedroom."

Up I went, secretly slightly chuffed that Mummy/Sue was still needed, and there, on the wall by my bedroom at the top of the stairs was a definite outline of a man. He had longish hair and a beard, and had rather an Elizabethan air about him. He was seated at an old fashioned writing desk or table, and you could actually see the movement of the quill pen he was holding. And lo, the moving finger writes!

I calmed them down and I think managed to convince them that it was a trick of the light although Gaby especially was evermore slightly wary in that house. I tried every which way to work out how it got there and never came up with a satisfactory explanation.

The house we lived in at that time was a 1930's sturdy, no-nonsense brick detached house just down from the Crooked Billet on Wimbledon Common. I knew the history of the house. The woman we bought it from had grown up there, her parents having lived in it from new, and when her father died she and her husband bought it from her mother, so no skeletons in that closet. But there must have been plenty lurking elsewhere and they missed no opportunity to make their presence felt. I have since lived in an early Victorian house and then in a house which is part Tudor and part Queen Anne, but I can honestly say I've never had as many ghostly happenings as in that one.

One of my very good friends is called Bobbie, a vivacious little Scots lady with a great sense of fun. Her father was a very gifted medium back in Edinburgh, and Bobbie has inherited his talent, although she rarely uses it. I also had the perfect lodger for many years called John Lavers. He became a very close friend of the family, and lived with us from Monday to Friday for many years, working in London and going back to his family in Devon at the weekend. In fact, he even moved house with us a couple of times.

The front door was, to the uninitiated, practically impossible to open and had to be closed with an almighty slam. One day, Bobbie and I were sitting in the breakfast room enjoying a long, gossipy lunch when we heard the front door open and close – well, you couldn't really miss it! We then heard heavy footsteps stomping up the stairs.

"It must be John back from work early," I said. I was a little concerned because he always stuck his head round the door to say hello, plus he followed his routine like clockwork and it was unheard of for him to get home so early unless smitten with beriberi. "I had better go and see if he's okay."

When I went to check, there was absolutely no sign of John anywhere and no trace of anyone else in the house. I went back to Bobbie and we decided it must have been a noise outside.

About five minutes later the same thing happened. Crash went the door, stomp went the footsteps. Suddenly, from Lulu's bedroom, which was directly above the breakfast room, came the most God awful racket. It sounded as if the room was being ransacked, with drawers being pulled out, cupboards tipped over, and books and ornaments being hurled around. Bobbie and I looked at each other.

"We'd better go and look," she said in a tiny voice.

Now, I am only five foot three and Bobbie is even smaller, and in those days we were quite skinny, so we weren't exactly a match for a big, burly burglar. Arm in arm, clutching onto each other for dear life, we crept up the stairs, hearts beating nineteen to the dozen, terrified of what we would find. We tiptoed along the corridor to the bedroom door, the noise becoming louder as we got nearer. I slowly turned the handle and, knees knocking like castanets, pushed the door open. Nothing! Not a sign of anything untoward! The room was exactly as it had been earlier that morning.

"Och, that's alright then," said Bobbie. "It's only a ghost."

"What a relief," I replied, and we went down to finish lunch. Ghosts we could deal with.

Apart from the dining room, of which there's more later, Lulu's room seemed to attract activity. It was not unusual when sitting on the terrace to look up and see a figure looking back at you, although to my mind, it would have been an intrepid ghost who would face the assortment of small furry mammals, terrapins, and canaries that lived in her sitting room area.

As she was getting ready for school one morning, she said to me, "Why did you walk into my room in the middle of the night?"

"I didn't," I answered, and then the pre-school scramble took over. It was only recently that she told me she had seen a woman in a grey dress with a fitted bodice and long skirt like a fin-de-siècle governess walk across her room and straight out of the window. Not something I'm prone to do. When I asked her why she hadn't said anything, her reply was, "Well, Mummy, things like that are so commonplace, we don't really notice them that much."

CHAPTER 3

Life in the eighties was very interesting for a well-off single woman in her thirties, with the added cachet of already having bagged a husband. However, being back on the dating scene after thirteen years was daunting. The world had moved along apace and men no longer felt obliged to declare undying love to get your knickers off. So far, pas de problème! My *problème* was that once they did tell me they loved me and wanted to marry me, I tended to believe them, and consequently, much of the early eighties were spent lurching from one romantic disaster to another.

I was in the hairdresser's one day when the woman next to me started to tell the assembled company about this terrific medium she had been to see. Going to my hairdresser's was like being at a never-ending party, helped along by vast quantities of alcohol that was ordered as take-away from the posh hotel across the road. You really had to time your run with certain stylists and get your hair done before too many tequilas had been quaffed, or the results could be a little cutting-edge to say the least.

Anyway, there we were, chatting and sipping, when my neighbour said that she had been to see this amazing guy called Stephen Speed. My lovely camp hairdresser let out a squeal, "Darling, you ought to see him. Your life is such crap. He may be able to sort you out. God knows, none of the rest of us can."

All eyes turned expectantly to the no-hoper with the head full of foils. "Um, okay," I mumbled. "Give me his number."

I rang Stephen and made an appointment, and one sunny afternoon I negotiated the unknown territory around the back of Olympia, found the address, and rang the bell.

The door was opened by a tall, dark, good-looking Australian. "Hi, I'm Stephen. Come on up."

On meeting Stephen, one could not have guessed he was gay – which must have been a disappointing revelation to quite a few young ladies – but once I got to his flat, I got a pretty shrewd idea. His taste in ornaments was, shall we say, exotic, and I was always quite riveted by a pencil sharpener that left little to the imagination.

He made us a cup of tea, we made sure we were sitting comfortably, and then he began.

"Who's Emily?"

"She's my grandmother."

"I've got her surrounded by baskets of flowers. Not vases, baskets." "She was a florist with Moyse Stevens."

"I'm getting a most peculiar message. I really don't know what it means. She's saying, 'Yes, I pushed her'."

Well, I nearly fell off my chair!

My darling Gran was born in 1888, the third of four sisters all born under the sign of Scorpio. Kate, Alice, Emily and Evie, who all lived to ripe old ages, except for "poor Evie who went so young" at the tender age of eighty-six. She met Grandpa and they started stepping out together when they were eighteen. Theirs was a blissfully happy marriage until Grandpa's comparatively premature death at fifty-eight from leukemia. Gran had kept the letters they had sent to each other over the years on the odd occasions they had been separated, and the letters written just before his death were still as romantic as those of young lovers. She was heartbroken when he died and she never stopped loving him over the next thirty-three years. I was born two weeks after his death and she instantly formed a bond with me, maybe finding a small comfort in the new, first grandchild.

She was a large, extremely well-corseted lady, always immaculately hatted and gloved with a discreetly powdered nose. She had a terrific sense of humour and when something amused her she would laugh silently, shaking like a jelly with tears of mirth streaming down her cheeks. She was a brilliant mimic and, although she had never had a piano lesson in her life, could play anything by ear. Her speciality was old Musical Hall songs, which she taught me. This stood me in very good stead in the days of post-war rationing. One day in the butcher's queue, aged about four, I gave a rousing rendition of:

"Lottie Collins' got no drawers. Will you kindly lend her yours? If you don't, she'll have to play with a tarararaboomdiay!"

Interspersed with, "May I have some liver for my tea, please?" Worked a treat and maybe explains why I have been singing for my supper ever since!

Gran, Mummy, Daddy and I lived in a rented Victorian semi. Gran occupied the top two floors, and the rest of us were on the ground and first floors. Gran was my rock, my comfort, my security, story-teller par excellence, and terrific puller-outer of wobbly first teeth. Without her, my memories of childhood, and maybe my teeth, would have been very different.

I loved her to bits and spent many happy hours with her, playing pirates, turning her table upside down to make a boat, tea cosy on my head, brandishing her large wooden spoon as a sword. Another time it would be hospitals with our Labrador in the role of patient. He'd be stretched out on the sofa, dressed in my old pyjamas and covered with the green baize, being fed medicine made from aniseed balls soaked in water. Says a lot for the dog! One day he escaped and made a bolt for it, pink brushed flannel flapping in the breeze, and chased by my extremely embarrassed mother.

Every Sunday evening, I would be washed, brushed and put into a clean dress, and we would, rather formally, climb the stairs to Granny's for high tea. Somehow, I remember we always had something with celery, followed by fresh cream meringues – a treat indeed in those early post-war years – and we listened to *Journey Into Space* on the wireless. What with the excitement and suspense engendered by the adventures of Mitch, Lemmie and Co., plus the cream, I always went to bed feeling slightly, but rather pleasantly, sick.

Luckily for me, I had Gran, because my mother was a ghastly woman over whom we will shortly draw a veil. When I was eleven, the occasion to buy the house arose. My parents thought it an excellent opportunity as they could buy at a low price because Gran was the sitting tenant, and so they could resell almost immediately for a handsome profit. Although the lease was in Gran's name, she didn't seem to have much input in all this. My mother did say grudgingly that Gran could move with us if she wanted. Gran's pride kicked in big time and, with great dignity, she swept off to live with her sister, Kate, and niece at Bexhill-on-Sea in Sussex until her daughter, my Auntie Joan, and her family came back from Singapore where they had been stationed for several years. Gran looked very like the old actress Margaret Rutherford and could "sweep" rather well. Mummy and Gran had always hated each other, but Gran had been too much of a lady to do anything overtly, although I do remember her giving me half a crown to buy a kitten from the local pet shop after hearing Mummy say that if we got a cat she would leave home!

Aunt Kate had an enormously loud, deep voice which would have put a Grenadier Guards RSM to shame. The two old ladies used to love to watch television together and they were particularly fond of watching a piano player called Russ Conway, who was very popular in the sixties, and famed for his gleaming teeth and beaming grin. Aunt Kate was always convinced he was smiling at her personally and would get quite fluttery during his shows. One day, as they were watching Russ smile at Aunt Kate, a Cavalier walked through the wall, saw the two old ladies, stopped, doffed his hat, bowed deeply, and walked straight in front of the television and through the opposite wall.

"I say, Emily," Aunt Kate boomed at Gran. "Did you see that?"

"Yes," replied Gran. "Nice young man, wasn't he?" and back they went to watching Russ and his smile.

For the last six years of her life Gran was bedridden, although her mind was still as sharp as a razor. Which is worse? To be trapped in a body with a failing mind, or to retain all one's faculties but be trapped in a body that is ceasing to function? My aunt was a true angel, nursing her uncomplainingly for all those years, although the burden of invalidity weighed heavily on Gran.

She didn't fear death, having a very strong faith and unswerving belief that she would be reunited with Grandpa. When she was ninety-one, she got pneumonia. She was rushed to the hospital where she was resuscitated and, in spite of the excellent care given to her in Crawley General, she passed a difficult and painful six weeks until her death.

The last time I saw her she was very weak and said to me, "Darling, I'm scared. I don't think I'm going to see Grandpa."

This sent a chill through me. She had always had such faith in the Hereafter and it broke my heart to think of my darling Gran feeling alone and afraid.

I was even more heartbroken when she died, and sobbed loudly and productively all through the funeral. I was still sobbing when we got back to my aunt's house for the funeral tea, and was patted, mopped, and supported by my poor, long-suffering cousin Richard. My mother was ahead of us, blithely tripping up the path as if it were a garden party, when she stumbled slightly – probably due to the presence of the emergency bottle of gin in her handbag. She regained her balance and then suddenly shot forward, arms akimbo, to land face down in the lobelia. Richard and I looked at each other.

"Good God!" he said. "The old girl's pushed her."

We had talked about this over the years and were both convinced that mother's descent into the flower beds was due to Gran's ghostly hand.

So, dear reader, you can imagine how freaked out I was to get Stephen's strange message: "Yes, I pushed her."

The second time I went to see Stephen, he said, "Do you know anybody called Daphne?"

"No."

"I'm getting a very strange name. Diaphanous? Adolphus? What sort of a name is that?"

"That's my grandfather."

He rejoiced in the name of Adolphus Henry Furneaux Hayman and when I was born, my parents decided to give me one of his names. I guess I was lucky to get Furneaux - Adolphusina Samuel could have been writing this!

"Well, he and Gran (by this time, she and Stephen were old friends) are standing very close together and your grandmother wants you to think back to the last conversation you had with her."

My mind went straight to the time when she spoke to me about her fears of never seeing Grandpa again and I was totally delighted that the two ever-young lovers were finally reunited. Gran still is my rock, my comfort, and my security. Luckily, I haven't yet had to put her to the test about wobbly second teeth! As for the story telling, well, maybe this book is a result!

These two meetings with Stephen were my first actual contact with the spirit world. Over the years I have had other experiences, but nothing has impressed me as much. He was a truly lovely man with an exceptional gift. He once told me that, during a séance, he had died for twenty minutes. I have never sat in a circle or taken part in a proper séance, but I understand that it can be extremely dangerous for the medium. If he or she is in a very deep trance, any sudden loud noise or interruption can be fatal, and this is what happened to Stephen. One of the ladies in the circle was a nurse and she tried with all her might to bring him back. After about fifteen minutes, she gave up. Everyone was crying over the corpse when suddenly, it sat up, apparently none the worse for wear, although the same couldn't be said for the others! He told me he had been very aware of going towards some beautiful place when his guide, John, had appeared to him and told him to go back as it was not yet time. The reason he was out for so long was that he was having a huge argument with John and refusing to leave! Thank God John won and Stephen came back to us. Perhaps this experience is why he had such a hotline to the spirit world. I know that if I were only one-hundredth as talented as he, I would be proud.

He was an amazingly talented man and helped me tremendously to develop as a medium. He also got me through traumatic times, talking to me late at night when I was a snivelling wreck after another love affair had bitten the dust, and giving me hope for the future. I remember one day he said to me, "Darling, they are putting you through the fires of hell to forge you into steel."

I did ask if I could just be a bit of aluminium instead, but I don't think "they" were particularly amused.

One day, my husband John came to me during a sitting. Stephen said, "Your husband is here. He wants you to know he has built a beautiful Cape Cod style clapboard house for you, miles from anywhere, with deer and rabbits playing on the lawns. It can be just the two of you forever."

This did not provoke the reaction Stephen expected. "Where is he?" I shouted, eyes swivelling wildly.

"Er, behind your right shoulder." I swung round. "You bastard! You never wanted me to have friends when we were married and now you want to isolate me again. If you think you can buy me with bunnies, think on!"

When I got home, Lulu asked, "Hi, Mummy. How's Stephen? How did it go?"

"I've just had a terrible row with you father," I said, pouring a bucketful of wine. Not always easy being my daughter!

When John was alive, we were very friendly with a couple called Sue and Ian. He was a great character. In spite of being diagnosed with Hodgkinson's Disease at twenty, he had beaten that into remission and gone on to make a fortune. He and John had a lot in common, both with a South London background, both self-made men, and both with an insouciant disregard for authority. Very sadly, when Ian was in his late thirties, the cancer came back, coinciding with, through no fault of his own, his business going into liquidation. Ian was a fighter. He started up a brand new business while on chemotherapy, having to stop the car to throw up on his way to meetings, as he was determined not to let his wife and children suffer financially.

Sue was a slightly different kettle of fish. She was like the little girl with the little curl – when she was good she was very, very good, but when she was bad she was horrid! She could be your greatest strength and support, but could also suddenly turn. She didn't take too kindly to having a sick husband and comparatively little money, and did not bother to hide this from Ian who, by the time he died, had regained quite a lot of his fortune.

As the end grew near, Sue anticipated her freedom. We had a wonderful dress shop in Wimbledon Village, run by Dieter and Vincenzo. Whenever you went in it was a party, and even if you didn't buy anything, you had a great time. They were a truly simpatico couple.

Sue went in one day. Vincenzo enveloped her in a warm embrace. "Sue, Sue, cara mia. How are you? How is Ian?"

"I want a blouse for his funeral."

"Oh, Dio! Oh, no! Sue, I'm so sorry. When did it happen? When is the funeral?" "He's not dead yet, but I thought I'd get the outfit early as I want to look my best!"

After Ian died, Sue was left very well off, but proceeded to go through the hard-earned cash like a dose of salts, moving to Chelsea and spending inordinate amounts on custom-built cars and Lebanese toy boys. I had rather let the friendship slide but, after about eighteen months, she started to leave loads of messages on the answerphone, most of which I ignored. However, one day I switched the machine on to hear, "It's me. You're the only person who can help me. I think I'm being haunted and I'm scared the kids' lives are in danger." That was one I couldn't refuse.

When I arrived at her smart new flat, she told me things were being moved around, especially photos of the children. I told her not to worry as it was probably only Ian making contact. With this, she leapt up like a scalded cat and let out a shriek. A guilty conscience is an amazing thing because she was absolutely petrified about Ian's reaction to her pre and post-mortem behaviour. I reassured her that once someone crossed into spirit, they became sweetness and light and only wanted to look after us, and she calmed down.

Just after this, I had one of my meetings with Stephen. "Your husband is here and he has brought a friend. They had a lot in common and were both ill at the same time, although this man had something wrong with his lungs." True. "He has a dog with him, a Springer Spaniel called Timmie."

They did indeed have a Springer called Timmie for a short time, and Ian was very attached to him. However, dogs were only ever transient visitors in that household and I think Timmie went away prematurely to that great dog's home in the sky.

"He wants to thank you for being so kind to Sue and the children at his funeral." "Oh, it was nothing. Least I could do."

"He wants you to give her a message." "Of course I will."

Stephen's flat was very dark and chock-a-block with furniture. It had a rather brooding, slightly spooky air made even more disconcerting by the homoerotic art and "sculptures" adorning every surface.

Suddenly, in a quavering, unearthly voice, Stephen began to sing, "We'll meet again, don't know where, don't know when, but I know we'll meet again some sunny day."

Needless to say, I didn't pass on the message!

As I said earlier, he made no secret of the fact that he was gay, and one day I asked him what he thought heaven was like.

"Darling," – his sentences were always prefaced with 'darling' – "My idea of heaven is a gay ski slope with everlasting powder snow."

The first day I met him, when he opened the door to me, I saw, in blue letters above his head, the letters A.I.D.S. This was the early eighties, just after the first AIDS victim had died and we then, in our wisdom, thought it was just a disease that attacked gay men. Anyway, I thought

I was going a bit mad and then forgot about it in the excitement of meeting Gran.

Just after my fortieth birthday, I called him in a bubble of excitement, just having met a "wonderful man".

"Hi, sweetie. Can I come and see you?"

"Yes, of course, but I must warn you, I haven't been very well." "What's wrong?"

"They are talking about AIDS."

Now in those ignorant days, I had always thought I would run a mile from anyone who had it, but when I went to see Stephen and he opened the door to me looking so frail and ill, with lesions on his beautiful face, I just hugged him. I was so sad when he died, but take great comfort from the thought of him skiing off-piste in the day, and on the piss in the evenings, doing all the "naughty things" he used to enjoy so much. He was a very special man with a very special gift. God bless you, Stephen.

CHAPTER 4

The eighties were a time of having it all. We were told that women had the right to high-flying careers and the perfect family. We were expected to be cordon bleu cooks and the happy recipients of a couple of dozen earth-moving orgasms a week. Magazines and self-help books bombarded us with examples of thin, glamorous women who had achieved Nirvana.

Money was plentiful. We shopped, lunched, and complained about the mostly long-suffering au pairs who took over much of our domesticity. We partied hard, drank ourselves silly, and then whipped our abused bodies back into submission with punishing Jane Fonda workouts. Unfortunately, most of the women I knew had neither careers nor the perfect family. With a couple of glaring exceptions, we all cooked reasonably well, but there was definitely a dearth in orgasms!

Desperate to be beautiful, we spent a huge amount of time and money at hairdressers, beauty salons, and health farms. Desperate to be loved, like moths drawn to the flame, we batted from one clairvoyant to another in the hope that the spirit world would rescue us from rather loveless marriages contracted in an era when the greatest disgrace was to be left on the shelf.

At this time, interest in star signs, horoscopes, and fortune telling was cracking on apace. One of the first questions you were asked at a cocktail party was what your star sign was. Whenever I said I was a

Scorpio, I used to get the reply, "I used to be married to a Scorpio." Strangely, nobody still was!

My friend Patti, a beautiful blonde six-foot-tall Amazon with a personality to match. She specialised in finding new clairvoyants, hoping against hope to find one who would tell her that, with a wave of a magic wand, her unhappy marriage to a perfectly nice but dim insurance broker would disappear and Prince Charming would charge into the rescue.

We used to escape from time to time and seek sanctuary from motherhood at a spa near Newbury. During one visit, they had a resident medium called Christian, and so, naturally, Patti and I made appointments to see him. He was spookily accurate and so I carried on seeing him back in London.

I also recommended him to several friends, including a lovely gay guy called John Mason, who ran a very successful catering business. Anyway, John went along to see him, and for Christian it was a coup de foudre! He fell madly in love, but unfortunately for him it was unreciprocated as John was already in a strong, loving relationship.

Being a Yorkshireman, Christian did not give up easily, even getting a woman friend to try to intercede on his behalf. Eventually John rang me in a panic.

"I can't dodge him anymore. He's desperate for me to have dinner with him. You've got to come with me!"

"When and where are we going?" "Tomorrow evening. Ménage à Trois." Where else?

"I'll pick you up at eight o'clock."

Ménage à Trois was a fashionable restaurant in London's Knightsbridge. It had a live pianist, and was one of the front runners in the nouvelle cuisine movement; a clever concept as I was always amazed at how much money could be charged for so little food. The wine was a rather violent yellow, and rejoiced in the name of "Clochemerle", a total joy for those familiar with the hysterically funny French story about the attempts of a small village of that name to get a pissoir installed.

Off we went to be greeted by Christian, resplendent in an elegantly cut double-breasted pink tweed suit and sporting diamond earrings that I would have given my eye teeth for!

John was frozen, like a rabbit in the car headlights. "Pretend we're a couple," he hissed.

Oh God!

All through dinner, John kept cuddling me and calling me darling, but I don't think he was very convincing as the other diners were quite mesmerised by our little trio, obviously trying to work out who was who, and who did what to whom.

During his reading, Christian had told John that he (John) would fall in love with a Libran. Emboldened by copious amounts of Clochemerle, John asked him his star sign.

"I'm not telling you," replied Christian.

"I bet you're a Libran." I giggled inanely. "Who have you been talking to?"

"No-one," we chorused, denying any interrogation of the female go-between. "We just guessed."

"You're telling porky pies," said Christian in a sepulchral voice, and with that he cast his eyes down, raised them to the ceiling, and lowered them again. As he did so, the restaurant lights dimmed, came back on, and dimmed again. John and I were petrified. When Christian went off to the loo, he left his handbag on his chair. We gazed, hypnotised.

"Don't say a word," said John in a stage whisper. "He's probably got us bugged!"

Needless to say, the affair never got off the ground, but I reckon we should have had a discount from the restaurant for providing the cabaret that night!

Christian continued to flourish as a clairvoyant, and my friend Diana consulted him for many years. However, he became very expensive, charging £80 for half an hour, which was a huge amount of money in those days. The last time Di went to see him, all he said was, "Tell Sue

Perry this, tell Sue Perry that." That was my name before I got married again.

"Blimey!" said Diana to me later. "I think that's a bit much. Eighty quid to be told <u>your</u> future."

One day Patti rang me, gibbering with excitement, to tell me she had discovered the most amazing clairvoyant called Ada Caesar. Impressed with what she had told Patti, I dutifully trotted off to Mrs. Caesar. She was a wonderful old Cockney woman who admitted to being ninety-three. According to the rather elderly lady who worked in the local florist, old Ada was lying about her age as she had known Mrs. C from being a tiny girl and she was much older than that. Way to go, girl!

Mrs. Caesar was a medium, a healer, and a very talented clairvoyant who had worked with the police on several cases. I went to see her one day and she was very disturbed by a vision she had had of a plane crashing into a remote village and killing hundreds of people. This was about three weeks before the Pan Am flight crashed into the village of Lockerbie in Scotland.

If you were troubled, she would press bits of rag into your hand as you left, saying.

"'Ealing thoughts, darlin'. Keep them with you," and somehow you felt better.

She also had a slightly more robust attitude to life. Patti went to see her in a terrible state.

"Oh, Mrs. Caesar. I'm so unhappy. I just can't stop crying." "Never mind, ducks. The more you cry, the less you piddle!"

She actually spent a lot of her time fighting evil, which I only discovered after one slightly unfortunate experience.

I met my friend Allie when I went to get my hair coloured for the first time in Harrods hairdressing salon. I didn't have a clue which stylist to pick, so I just told them I wanted the one with the beautiful red hair. We clicked straight away, and by the time I left, with stylish burgundy streaks in my hair, we had become firm friends. She was a psychic power house, but had absolutely no control over it. She was wide open for any mischievous spirit to take advantage. One night at about 3a.m. I got a phone call. "It's me."

"God, it's 3a.m. Are you okay?" "There's someone in the house." "Have you called the police?" "Not that sort of someone."

The voice sounded strangely muffled. "Are you having some sort of attack?"

"No. I'm hiding under the duvet. Come and do something."

So, I got into the car and drove to Ealing to find a quaking Allie, and a mischievous little man with tufty white hair and twinkly blue eyes, sporting a rather startling pair of check trousers and a cutaway coat. He thought it great sport to appear and disappear from the feet up, leaving just a big smile like the Cheshire Cat.

"I don't know what's wrong with your friend," he said. "I don't think she can take a joke."

When I explained to him how much he was freaking her out, he apologised profusely, bowed, and faded gracefully, grin and all.

Allie and I were becoming more and more fixated on contacting the other side. Neither of us really knew what we were doing, but we were getting rather cocky about the whole thing, and entirely unaware of what we could stir up.

One of the most dangerous things one can do is mess around with a Ouija board. I must say here that I am not very knowledgeable about the ins and outs of the spirit world, but I have been told that when you die, the better person you have been, the higher the astral plane you go to. If you are a real nasty, you end up on the lower astral planes or, as dear old Mrs. Caesar would say, "'E's stuck in the astrals, ducks," - a condition that sounded remarkably painful. The reason most mediums have a spirit guide is literally to be guided through the dark regions of "the astrals" to the nice souls on the higher planes. If you play around with a Ouija board, you cannot easily get through the lower planes and often end up contacting someone you would rather not have popping in for a chat and a cup of tea.

My mother was the first one to tell me about Ouija boards. I must mention here that she thought she was a witch (I'm serious!) and after she started watching *Bewitched* on the television, there was no stopping her. That nose would wrinkle at the drop of a hat, causing her to look like a startled rabbit.

She worked in a small office in Regent Street with three or four other women. One day, their bosses away, they decided to have a go at summoning up spirits using a glass. They nipped down to the basement where a lot of old furniture and pictures were stored, and gathered round a small table with the paraphernalia set up on it. Mummy, being chief coven bunny, asked, "Is anybody there?"

"Yes," came the reply.

"Who is it?" trilled Mummy in a state of great excitement. "The Devil." This was unexpected.

"Alright," said my mater disbelievingly. "If you are the Devil, give us a sign."

At that moment a huge ornate mirror resting against one wall cracked completely in two from top to bottom. Coincidence? All I know is that you don't mess with Old Nick.

Having heard this story on numerous occasions, I was sceptical but intrigued. When I was eighteen, my friend Sandy and I knew a group of boys who lived in Essex. They were not boyfriends, just friends who happened to be boys. They were very handy escorts and good mates.

My parents went on holiday to Tunisia and Sandy came to stay with me. We invited two of the boys, Roddy and Dave, over to supper. After dinner we got talking about Mummy's encounter with Lucifer and somebody, probably me, suggested we have a go ourselves.

Slightly self-conscious, we set up the table and put our fingers on the glass. It started moving.

"Okay, who's pushing?" I asked. The other three took their hands away. Mine was the only finger left and the glass was still moving.

"Who's there?" we asked, a little nervously. At first it spelt out nonsense, but then it wrote Mary Smith, an innocent enough sounding name.

"Do you have a message for anyone?" "Yes, for Roddy."

"What is your message?"

By this time Sandy was writing down what the glass spelt out. The glass was moving at a rate of knots and Sandy went pale as she read out what had been given to us. "And who doth with us walk through the valley of the shadow of death!" We panicked. We each had a large slug of my father's best brandy. After a while, fortified by one sort of spirit, I suggested having a go at contacting the other again. After all, we couldn't possibly get the same spirit – could we?

We did. Up popped Mary. Again, we asked if she had a message for anyone and again came the same answer: Roddy.

"What is your message?" we asked. The glass went mad. PXZQCR.

"Why won't you tell us your message?" I asked. The glass moved again. This time it spelt out: "We cannot tell, we can only kill."

We were thoroughly spooked. We hastily put the glass away and, just as hastily, reached for the brandy bottle. Sandy and I were so scared we wouldn't let the boys leave until it got light. This caused a few problems as the old biddy next door was up and peering through the net curtains. As soon as my parents got back, she beetled round to tell them that men were seen coming out of the house at 5a.m.

Roddy had a darling little red sports car which was his pride and joy, and which he drove in true boy-racer style. Time passed and nothing more was heard from the boys. This was quite surprising as we had been pals, but I thought we had scared them off with our séance. Eventually, after a couple of years, I bumped into a mutual friend, Justine. We chatted and I said, casually, "Do you ever hear anything of Roddy?"

Justine went pale. "Haven't you heard?" She gasped. "Roddy disappeared."

What do you mean disappeared?" I was shocked. "People don't just disappear." "Well, he went out in his car one day and just … disappeared.

No trace was ever found of him or the car. Nobody knows what happened to him."

Mary Smith's words came flooding back to me: "And who doth with us walk through the valley of the shadow of death." Coincidence again?

But memories get blurred and forgotten over time, and fears soften and fade with the years. And so it was that one evening after a few buckets of Muscadet, Allie and I decided to have a go with our improvised Ouija board. It seemed like a good idea at the time and we did get a few answers to some simple questions, but suddenly the atmosphere became cold and heavy with malevolence. We were petrified. Suddenly stone cold sober, I managed to pull myself together and shouted at whoever was there to bugger off. That seemed to do the trick and, laughing somewhat sheepishly, we said goodbye and Allie drove home.

The next morning, she rang.

"Whoever it was came home with me in the car and is still here."

"Tell it to piss off."

"I have. It doesn't take any notice."

If this was the same presence, it was indeed scary. Time to call in the big gun. I called Mrs. Caesar.

"Mrs. C. I need to see you urgently. We may have raised something better left alone." Off I went to receive a right bollocking from Mrs. Caesar about messing around with Ouija boards, but she agreed to help. I don't know what she did, but she certainly got the presence on the run. Allie reported back that the atmosphere had lifted and the sense of evil had disappeared.

When I thanked Mrs. Caesar for helping, she said, "That's alright, ducks. I have to deal with a lot of this and much worse than this one, I can tell you. You wouldn't believe the problems I get from the Common."

I was intrigued. Most of my knowledge of the inhabitants of Wimbledon Common was restricted to the doings of the Wombles. Could it harbour more than Great Uncle Bulgaria and Madame Cholet in its bosky depths?

There is a place on Wimbledon Common called Caesar's Well, which is the site of an old Roman encampment. Mrs. Caesar (no relation as far as I know) told me that during the forties and fifties it was decided to cover up the well as it posed a danger. She said that during the process of concreting over it, quite a few of the workmen met untimely deaths and, spiritually, it was not at all a good area.

"There's a Black Magic Circle meets there and I have to sort quite a few things out from that. I get people knocking on my door at all hours."

The thought of Mrs. C in her nightie and hair net, tussling with the Devil on her doorstep is one to be treasured.

She told me there was a large group of Satanists active in Wimbledon, their numbers swelled by a certain sector of the gay community who also met on the Common and who were drawn to the idea of the occult. I took this with a pinch of salt, but she told me quite matter-of-factly that the High Priestess was "that woman who is the matron of a care home and lives in ****** Street." As we talked further, I began to realise that Dennis Wheatley's book *The Devil Rides Out* wasn't so far-fetched after all.

I must say that after that, I steered clear of the area around Caesar's Well and never more felt quite the same about Tobermorey and Co.

CHAPTER 5

People often ask me how you can have a reading that tells you something and then, maybe a year later, have another that tells you something completely different. The only explanation I can think of is that I see paths ahead. I can tell you what path you are on at the time of the reading. I can tell you of good times ahead so you may profit from this information, and I can tell you of bad times so you can take evasive action, but there is one thing I cannot factor into the equation, and that is free will. We come to crossroads and we choose the fork to take. Sometimes it is the path we are meant to tread, sometimes not, and sometimes a very determined spirit world will guide us back onto that path like sheep dogs herding their flock into the fold.

Mary West, Queen of Poodleland, had been right with both readings. When I first went to her she had foreseen 'the rocky road ahead' and then the rich, charming older man who would love me and want to marry me. The second time I consulted her, my path had changed – thank God, as it turned out.

Laurie and I gave a New Year's Eve party and everyone, me included, was expecting the engagement to be announced, but instead, he dropped me in a very painful and public way at a lunch party the following day. I found this almost unbearable. It was like being widowed twice in two years. Somehow, I soldiered on until Valentine's Day. The enormity of loss, plus an evil mother-in-law who had started court proceedings to try and do me out of my inheritance the day John died, all proved too much. I ceased to function. I had coped reasonably bravely with John's death and hadn't really cried that much, but then I sure made up for it. My lovely and much too handsome doctor, Tim, was called. He took one look at the sobbing wreck in front of him and immediately dispatched me to the local nursing home where I was knocked out for a couple of days and then force-fed like a Strasbourg goose. The one good thing, in my opinion, to come out of all this was that I had, for the first time in my life, got thin. When I was better, I went into Harrods dress department. The assistant took one look at me and said, "Sorry, Madam. We haven't got anything small enough for you."

I whooped with delight. "Would you mind writing that down, please?"

This was long before the days of size zero.

Anyway, after a couple of days of medically induced snoozing and non-medically induced snivelling, self-preservation kicked in big time. I felt I had reached a total nadir and was damned if I was going to stay there.

At the time I had a wonderful au pair called Mercedes, a tiny, drop-dead gorgeous Spanish girl with huge grey eyes, a cloud of black curls, and a voice that outdid Lauren Bacall. She was sex appeal on a plate, and if I could have bottled whatever she had, I would have made a fortune. She always wore shoes a couple of sizes too big, like Minnie Mouse, and on this particular occasion I heard her unmistakable footsteps clomping down the corridor towards my room.

Never being one to do things by halves, I shot bolt upright in bed.

"Get out the summer clothes," I screeched. "We are going to Barbados next week!" And we did!

It was a great adventure. I had been to Antigua for my honeymoon in 1968, when life on the islands was very gentle, trusting and unspoilt, but by the early eighties, cheap flights and package holidays had brought tourism accompanied by a large dose of cynicism. It was a haven for well off 'cougars' and the local gigolos did a roaring trade, not making life easy for two pretty young women on their own with a rapidly developing ten-year-old. Luckily, our knight in shining armour appeared in the guise of a huge Bajan taxi driver who undertook the role of guardian and bodyguard, and showed us safely round the island.

There was a really nice couple staying at our hotel called Carol and Basil. They were middle-aged honeymooners, married later in life as it had taken Carol fifteen years to prise Basil away from his mother. They befriended us, and one day Carol confided in me that Basil was not his real name; he had changed it from Cecil! Go figure!

Our last day dawned. We were flying out late that evening so had another full day to enjoy the sunshine. We had arranged to meet Carol and Basil for a farewell lunch. Lulu and Mercedes had gone ahead and as I went to join them, I stopped to watch the waves which were incredibly high that day. Suddenly I heard a dark brown voice with an American accent say, "High seas today." I turned to see a small, elderly man with a clipped jet black moustache, immaculately turned out in white ducks and sporting a white captain's hat. "Will you do me the honour of lunching with me?"

Well, I was a bit taken aback, but assumed he was a lonely old guy in need of company. "That's very kind of you, but I'm on my way to meet friends. Maybe you would care to join us."

"With great pleasure, my dear. My name is Leonard Horowitz from Washington DC."

He offered me his arm, and Leonard Horowitz and I strolled into the beachside restaurant, much to the surprise of the assembled company.

During our week in Barbados, I had heard odd rumours about the UK's problems with Argentina. Having been rather cut off from news from home, I casually mentioned at lunch that I thought we might be at war. No-one seemed to know anything about this.

That afternoon, whilst we were packing, the phone rang.

"I have rung the Pentagon, my dear. Unfortunately, your country is at war with Argentina." Well, that was service for you!

We had not been back in England for long – just long enough for me to get my hair done as my beautiful burgundy streaks had turned orange in the Caribbean sun – when, late one night, the telephone rang. I picked it up, wondering who could be calling at such a late hour.

"This is your admirer from across the Potomac." "Who?"

"Leonard Horowitz, my dear." You could hear the moustache twirling. "Hello, Mr. Horowitz. What a surprise. How are you?"

"I am very well, my dear, and I am coming to Europe." "How nice."

"I would like you to book me into a very good hotel in London and then hope you would do me the honour of accompanying me to the South of France for a small vacation."

Was this guy for real?

Now, bear in mind I thought Mr. Horowitz was old, rather infirm and in need of a companion, so I booked him into the Dorchester. In my innocence, I thought a week on the French Riviera might be nice, especially if I could tuck my charge up in bed at 9.30 with a cup of cocoa. However, the thought crossed my mind that he could be a fortune-hunter or a mass-murderer, so I got my long-suffering solicitor to set the detectives on him. It is terrifying how much information you can get about a person. Within a week, I had his bank balance, social security number, and God knows how much more information, including the facts that he was single, lived in the infamous Watergate Building and was only in his mid-fifties. Still, that seemed very old to me at the time.

Mr. Horowitz duly arrived and I went up to London to meet him for dinner. In those days, I used to leave my car in Chelsea and then get a cab to wherever I was going in central London. He was a charming and erudite companion but, just as we were having coffee, he took my hand and took my breath away.

"My dear," he said. "I have been very successful in my life. I have made a lot of money (true), I have a wonderful apartment (true), and a very valuable art collection that I have built up over the years (also true). The only thing missing from my life is a beautiful wife and daughter. I would like to marry you and take you and Luisa back to live with me in Washington.

I was so gobsmacked that I actually heard myself saying, "Oh, Mr. Horowitz, this is so sudden."

"I will give you time to think about it, and, by the way, call me Leonard."

We finished dinner. I was still in a state of shock.

"I have presents for you and Luisa back at the hotel. Will you come and collect them?"

I weighed this up. Would it be too churlish to refuse? I should be alright if I lurked at the door and, after all, he was old!

We got to the room. Somehow, he shepherded me inside and then he pounced! I squeaked and ran round the other side of the room. He hurdled the bed in one bound.

"Oh, Mr. Horowitz, you are very fit!" I gasped as I neatly avoided his grasp.

"I play a lot of tennis. Call me Leonard, my dear." He leapt across the bed again, and again, I dodged him. We kept this silent-movie charade up for a few more minutes until I managed to reach the safety of the corridor. He had obviously given up for the time being. He gave me a large, beautifully gift-wrapped present for Lulu and a Yves Saint Laurent carrier bag for me.

"I will ring you tomorrow for your answer, my dear." Oh God!

"Goodnight, Mr. Horowitz, and thank you very much for dinner," I said politely. "Call me Leonard, my dear."

He put me in a taxi and, clutching my goodies which turned out to be a gorgeous Saint Laurent shawl and a very expensive children's painting, I gave the driver directions to the road where I had parked my car.

"Successful evening was it, darlin'?" asked the driver.

"I beg your pardon?" "Business good then, was it?"

God help us, the driver thought I was a high class hooker! "Please just take me to my car," I croaked.

"Tell, you what, luv, we can come to a little arrangement and I'll waive the fare."

By this time, I was getting hysterical. Luckily, we got to my car. I flung money at the driver and quickly locked myself in, safe at last.

The next day, Mr. Horowitz called me for my answer. I had to tell him that I was no longer able to accompany him to the South of France and that, with regret, I had to refuse his proposal of marriage. He went back to Washington and I went back to Wimbledon.

Mercedes eventually had to go back to Spain – a great loss for us, but not so for her as she was having a raging affair with the number one Spanish DJ at that time. And then, one magic day, into our lives came the divine Drea from Munich. Over the years she has been our Mary Poppins, and Lulu and I love her. She is family and one of our closest people, but God help me if she ever decides to divulge some of my secrets!

Anyway, having got a taste for the Caribbean, the three of decided to go to St Lucia. The hotel was a little like a holiday camp, but great fun nonetheless. One morning Drea and I were making our way to the pool when I suddenly clutched her.

"Oh my God!" I squawked. "It's Curt Jurgens!"

"I hope not," she replied laconically. "He's been dead for a couple of years."

I looked again. Tall, tanned, silver-haired and blue-eyed; the resemblance to the German actor was uncanny – and I've always been a sucker for blue eyes.

I smiled. He smiled back. Now in those days I wasn't bad looking and usually all it took was a smile. Not this time. The next day we exchanged 'good mornings'. Nothing. Nada. Zilch.

That evening, there was a cocktail party. I nonchalantly made my way across a crowded room. He was charming. He was from Zurich, divorced, and was on holiday with a couple of friends and his grown up sons. Rather unfortunately, he was called Cos, which made me think of lettuce. The party ended, he said au'voir and we went our separate ways.

This had now become a challenge. I wasn't used to not getting my man. As Cos and the gang spoke Suisse Deutch, it was impossible for me to casually break into the conversation.

Drea to the rescue. I walked into the bar one evening with Lulu to find Drea happily chatting with the group in German. We all spoke for a few minutes – in English – then Drea turned to Lulu. "Come, Lulu. Time for bed."

Luckily for me, Lulu was mute with shock. It was only 9.30p.m. but aided by sports instructor Drea's iron hand on the back of her neck, she went without a murmur, probably unable to speak on account of the head lock Drea had her in. I stayed put. What could they do but offer me a drink? I accepted gracefully. We chatted politely. Cos stood up, clicked his heels, and asked me if I would like to dance. I took Dr. Jekyll's hand and found myself in the arms of Mr. Hyde.

"Oh, darlink, darlink! I can't believe I've found you. You are so beautiful."

I felt as if I had slipped into a parallel universe. What the hell had they put in those rum punches?

"I'm leaving tomorrow," he continued. "How can I let you go?"

Definitely la la land, but very flattering and he was drop dead gorgeous. We strolled hand in hand along the moonlight strand, full of rum punches and unconsummated passion as, both being a bit stingy, we were sharing rooms with our entourages.

The next day, when he left, he cried. I breathed a sigh of relief. When I got back to Blighty, he bombarded me with beefcake photos of him in nothing but his budgie smugglers, and letters soaked in his aftershave, declaring undying love. I should have known better!

At that time, because of aforementioned mother-in-law, I had some money in a Swiss bank, all legal and tax paid, but out of the grasp of her sticky paws. Anyway, a bit bored and having received yet another missive from the lovelorn lettuce, I decided to check things out further.

I called him to say I was coming to Switzerland. "Oh, darlink! You are coming to Zurich to see me!"

Well, I didn't want him getting too cocky, so for some reason, I said I was going to Basel on business. Almost true as the bank was in Basel.

"What sort of business?" he asked.

"I'm sorry. Can't talk about it. Highly confidential."

In order to look the part of a mysterious, international business woman, I bought myself a red crocodile document case which contained nothing but copies of Vogue and L'Express, and which was always kept locked in case of stickybeaking. I put on my mink coat and highest heels and set off for my assignation.

We met at the Hotel Drei Konige, one of Europe's best hotels. Cos looked devastating in a very well-cut navy three-piece suit, and I had scrubbed up quite well. We dined by candlelight in the restaurant which is built out over the Rhine, the chemically murky waters below us given sparkle by the reflection of a myriad of lights.

I was in my element. Here was this gorgeous available man thinking I was the bees' knees. His sons sent their love, his friends sent their love, and even the 'formerly' wife sent her love. Then came the big mistake. I asked him what happened to his marriage.

His 'formerly' wife had had an affair with the sexy, handsome young guy who fixed her car.

"What did you do?" I asked.

"I sent her to a psychiatrist to see why she felt the need." Well, I could have told him that for free!

"The psychiatrist told her to do what she felt was right, so even though I bought a book and studied how to make love, she left me for him."

Oh God! In for a penny, in for a pound. He took my hand. "So what did you do?" We were speaking French at the time.

"J'ai fait un pélerinage."

I shook my head. I must have misunderstood. He went on a pilgrimage? "Do you mean a religious journey?"

"Yes. I was going to walk twenty kilometres in bare feet, but after one kilometre I couldn't go any further because my feet hurt, so I had to be carried home."

Quel héro! Quel wimp! I grabbed my hand back as if I had been burnt. I went straight off him. How was I going to survive the weekend? We went to our room. I had taken with me what was in those days a stylish vivid pink satin and lace nightie.

I was sitting up in bed, praying for a miracle when Cos appeared from the bathroom. He gazed at the vision in pink.

"Oh, darlink! You are so lovely. You look as if you are in the maternity hospital." That did it.

"Sleep on the couch," I said. "I have a terrible migraine."

Luckily I managed to swing that one for the whole weekend. I managed to survive all advances and even managed to survive the celebratory champagne the family provided to toast the next Frau Lettuce.

Sunday afternoon, migraine miraculously better, we got to the airport. Now, dear reader, here I must confess to a serious character flaw. I cannot resist playing a role. We got to passport control. Cos swept me into his manly arms.

"Darlink, do not go home. Stay here and marry me."

The whole airport was riveted. I was Suzanne Pleshette to his Troy Donahue.

Deep in character, I replied, "You know my responsibilities lie in England." By now I had morphed into Celia Johnson in *Brief Encounter*, nobly leaving behind love for duty.

I bravely tendered my passport. Cos cried, the passport official cried, the whole damn airport cried. Cos leaned over the barrier waving a sodden handkerchief until the escalator carried me to the safety of the departure lounge.

I boarded the plane, loaded the poor steward with all my stuff and sank gratefully into my seat.

"Would you like a drink, Madam?" asked the steward from behind my mound of belongings.

"God, yes! A glass of white wine please."

"Oh, no," said a gravelly, molasses voice next to me. "A lady like you must have champagne."

"Oh, shit!" I thought. "Not another one!" Then I turned to my right, and to my destiny for the next three years.

CHAPTER 6

I sometimes think of us mere mortals as chess pieces, moved around by giant immortal hands, rather like the Gods in *Clash of the Titans*. During all these romantic shenanigans I still kept beetling off to Stephen or Mrs. Caesar to find out what was going to happen to me. At other times the spirit world kept a rather low profile, although I now realise that Gran, John, Mrs. B and co. were there keeping an eye on me and pulling my strings occasionally, like benevolent puppeteers.

Anyway, arriving back from Basel, I somehow managed to get off the plane and back home, in spite of having virtually cleared British Airways out of champagne on the short flight home. Lovely Drea had been holding the fort. She opened the door and I wafted in.

"I met a lovely man," I purred dreamily, wafting fumes of alcohol and Chanel Number Five.

"I know," said a slightly bemused Drea. "You went out to meet him."

"No, not that one. Another one!"

His name was John Kyriakis; six foot four inches of arrogant Greek masculinity. The next three years were a real white knuckle ride. We dined, we danced, we drank champagne, and we travelled constantly all over Europe, fighting like cat and dog but making up memorably. I always insisted on buying my own plane ticket so I could leave whenever I wanted. I left him in restaurants, pretending to go to the ladies' room, secretly slipping out of the back door and home, but he always came after me, cursing me in Greek, but holding me tight.

We used to fly to Athens for the weekend. Kyriakis always insisted we flew Olympic Airways, not just because of nationalistic pride, but because he thought the stewardesses, in spite of, or maybe because of, a certain hirsuteness, were 'mutti figures' and would look after him well. We would get back on the plane on Sunday evening, laden with huge drums of olive oil and bags bulging with nuts, dried apricots, and honey. The motherly hosties would cluck and grumble slightly, but we always managed to bring back our excess of goodies.

Athens came as a real culture shock to me. I had expected another Rome, or Paris, or Madrid, but found myself in a quasi Middle Eastern metropolis. I had imagined I would be breaking my heels on ruins around every corner, but no. Apart from the Acropolis with its beautiful Parthenon, my impression was of a city of apartment blocks, rather like Beirut before the troubles.

But what a city of wonderful contrasts! We would often go to eat at a restaurant in the fishing port of Piraeus where we chose our dinner from a gleaming piscine cornucopia just unloaded from small fishing smacks. While we waited for our fish to be cooked, we drank rough local wine, seated on canvas and metal school chairs at oilskin covered tables. We were usually surrounded by mysterious dark men and glamorous, bejewelled women casually swathed in furs and cashmere, supremely elegant in a way only Southern European women seem to achieve.

We would then move on to expensive night clubs where singers entertained us, their lower bodies disappearing in a thick cloud of cigarette smoke which gave the impression of unearthly beings rising from an ethereal mist. It was the custom to buy flowers to throw at the singers in appreciation, which they, in turn, tossed back by way of a thank you, so that by the end of the evening every inch of flat surface was covered in petals. To this day, the smell of gardenias has the power to transport me straight back to those dimly lit rooms redolent with the perfume of flowers, smoke, and Retsina.

In retrospect, I think Kyriakis must have been a spy. There were mysterious trips to exotic places, bundles of cash everywhere, and unexpected properties all over Europe. He supposedly ran a small business making machine parts, but, by Jove, it must have been lucrative. He was obsessed with the KGB and was forever talking about them. He often went to Moscow where he and his friend Dimitri drank so much that he came back with raging gout, and laden with caviare and vodka which he would lovingly set out as if in the finest restaurant.

Phone calls from Russia in those pre-mobile phone days were not to be undertaken easily. One memorable day I was working at home when the phone rang. I picked up the receiver to hear a woman's voice saying, "Hello, London. Moscow calling."

Those of you who remember the Eurovision Song Contest will know what I mean when I say that I resisted the urge to reply, "Norvége nul point!"

When I met him he had separated from his wife. They still shared a house, but had separate living quarters. After he met me he moved out and got his own apartment, so I thought everything was kosher. Not long after we got together his old mother became very ill back in Athens, so he brought her over to England to spend her final days with her only son, and employed a full-time nurse to look after her. It was decided that I would steer clear of the flat in case my presence upset her. She was a bit rambling and thought he was still married.

A year after John died, before our trips to the Caribbean, my friend Sue decided that Lulu and I should go on a holiday. She took over the whole project and organised a week for us at the Grand Hotel Villa Serbelloni at Belaggio on Lake Como.

I'd wanted to go to Italy as I had spent a lot of time there when I was young. I'd spent the summers with friends of my parents, Signor Arturo and Signora Flora. My father, the dirty rat, had asked them to treat me as their own daughter, and as young Italian girls in the sixties had absolutely no freedom, I was kept on a very tight leash indeed. Whenever a young man came to take me out, Signora Flora, a large raw boned woman with sparse ginger hair, would appear. She would glare at the intrepid young man and her finger would start to wag.

"Suzi, stai brava!" (Be good, Suzi) "Stai attenta!" (Be careful)

"Non dimenticare, Suzi!" (Don't forget, Suzi)

By now the finger would be wagging out of control, and nine times out of ten I would be delivered home by 10p.m. One good thing to come out of this was that I learnt to speak Italian, and I also got a lot of sleep.

So, when Sue asked me where I would like to go, I immediately thought of Italy. It is my spiritual home, and many years later, when I came to live in Australia, I was not the least bit homesick for England, but yearned with all my heart to go back to Italy. Lulu and I set off to Belaggio, two rather scared little bunnies who had never before travelled on their own. The staff at the Villa Serbelloni were inordinately kind to us, taking care of us and tempting us with delicious food, and so, year after year we returned for a week in July.

The summer after I met Kyriakis, he had to go to Turin on business and we decided to combine that with our annual trip to Lake Como. Lulu and I arranged to meet him at the airport. When he arrived, he looked very flustered.

"Is something wrong?" I asked.

"The nurse walked out on me this morning. My mother thought she was a wolf!"

"What's going to happen?" I asked, digging Lulu hard in the ribs to stop her giggling.

"A neighbour is looking after her for me."

I didn't query this as my neighbours were all extremely supportive of each other.

We arrived at the Villa Serbelloni and were welcomed warmly by the concierge.

"Signora Perry, what a pleasure to see you and Luisa again."

I had booked in my name, but Kyriakis immediately altered the reservation to his. At the time, I took this to be merely a bit of machismo. We had a lovely week and I only found it slightly odd that he often had to go back to the room as soon as we settled down by the pool to make a 'business' call.

While we were on a boat trip, he changed the film in his camera and I put the old film in my bag. Now, my handbag is generally like a dustbin, and once things disappear into its murky depths, it often takes some time for them to resurface. A few weeks later, scrabbling through the detritus of my life, I found the film and decided to get it developed. I looked at the prints with my housekeeper, Mary. There were pictures of us in Italy, of his daughter at school in Switzerland, and of his mother with a rather plain, peroxide blonde woman of a certain age sporting turquoise crimplene and black horn-rimmed glasses. I assumed it was the neighbour who had stepped into the breach when the wolf left.

"I'm going to have some fun tonight," I said to Mary. "I'm really going to tease him about this."

Now this is where it gets a bit weird. It was 4th August, the anniversary of John's death, and it was pissing with rain. In fact, every 4th August the weather was terrible, so much so that my phlegmatic Yorkshire cousin refused to travel on that day as he swore John threw a tantrum each year about his sudden demise. Kyriakis and I were going for dinner to a Greek restaurant in North London, and by the time we got there we were soaked.

We got our drinks and ordered our food.

"Hey, Kyriakis," I said jokily. "Who's the blonde?"

He looked a bit shifty, but there was nothing unusual in that. This was, after all, the man who wrote down all the lies he told people in a little notebook so he could remember what he had told to whom.

"What blonde? I don't know any blondes."

"Well, she's with your mother by your swimming pool." "Oh! That's Joanna, my neighbour."

I had known that was who she was, but I felt there was something terribly wrong about the whole thing. I shivered. From somewhere, I heard myself saying, "You've had an affair with her."

His reply shook me to the core. "It depends on what you mean by an affair."

"And it's still going on," I whispered. Suddenly the unexplained business calls and the changed reservation became clear. The kindly neighbour was, in fact, his mistress.

I stood up and walked towards the door. I must have looked very fragile because I remember the waitress being so gentle with me as she draped my raincoat over my shoulders, as if I were made of glass and about to break at any moment.

What made me realise what was going on? I knew a neighbour was looking after his mother and, God knows, the woman didn't look like rival material. Why did it happen on John's anniversary?

Kyriakis and I got back together again after he had assured me that this woman was now history. Naturally, he was lying, and played us both like a couple of trout. Although her name was Joanna, I called her Doris. She was still married to a dentist and had five children. She made my life a misery, even getting her youngest son to make funny phone calls to me at odd hours. In fact, the situation got so bad that I had to get my solicitor to intervene.

Doris hated me and this manifested itself in a bizarre and terrifying way. In the midst of all this angst, I had to have a hysterectomy. In those days, this meant a long stay in hospital and, because I was on my own with Lulu, the doctors decided I should stay in for a fortnight. The day after the operation, the phone next to my bed rang. It was Doris. God knows how she had got the number, but she shouted abuse at me. I was still woozy with the anaesthetic and really couldn't cope with old Doris, so I told her in no uncertain terms to piss off.

Once the effects of the anaesthetic had worn off, it was really rather pleasant sitting up in bed, holding court in a room full of flowers and being waited on hand and foot. Towards the end of my stay, I was cosily tucked up in bed with a cup of cocoa. "This isn't bad," I thought to myself, and turned off the light, snuggling down under the covers. Immediately, I became aware of something in the corner of the room.

I don't know what it was, but there was a sense of pure evil emanating from it. I was paralyzed with fear. I tried to reach the buzzer to call the nurse, but I couldn't move a muscle. I opened my mouth to scream, but no sound came out. I tried to say the Lord's Prayer. I couldn't. All I could do was repeat over and over in mind, "Please, God, help me." Someone obviously heard my prayer because the thing gradually began to recede and I started to regain my faculties.

As soon as I could move, I switched on the light. Whatever it was had gone, literally thanks to God. Having talked to people much wiser than I in the ways of the occult, I understand there is something called a succubus which feeds off hatred, and I have come to the conclusion that some evil spirit had latched onto Doris' feelings towards me and launched an attack against me. Doris had certainly found a friend that night.

We soldiered on in this destructive fashion for about a year until I finally found the courage and self-respect to finish it, but I do wonder how long we would have gone on without husband John's divine intervention.

My lovely Gran was also pretty good at pointing the finger at any two timing varmints who happened to cross my path, and in the seventeen years between husbands, I sure met my fair share!

I was briefly engaged to a pilot I met at the Wimbledon Tennis Tournament. When we met, he had a big hole in his leg and was limping badly. For some reason, I got it into my head that he had been shot – something which at the time seemed very romantic – but the hole was due to a mosquito bite and the limp due to a knee twisted during a tennis match.

We were madly in love and whiled away many a happy hour discussing our future together. I knew he had always had an eye for a pretty woman, but so had I for a handsome man. We agreed our philandering days were over now we had found each other.

We were both, I thought, absolutely sincere in this belief, and I felt secure and happy. We lived in different parts of the country and didn't see each other that often. He used to go to Germany quite a lot on business and would always make a detour via Wimbledon on his way back.

One weekend, my parents had come to stay. This was never the easiest of times given Mummy's sharp tongue and attachment to the gin bottle, but I consoled myself with the thought that I would see Ray on Monday. On the Saturday at about 7.30p.m. I was in the kitchen peeling potatoes with Mummy talking at me when I suddenly saw the clearest scenario being played out in front of my eyes. I saw Ray at a formal dinner, sitting next to a pretty blonde woman, with all his RAF charm going into overdrive. I panicked!

"God, no! Gran, do something! Stop him!"

I felt a sort of whoosh, and Gran, aka Snagglepuss, exited stage right immediately.

On Monday, Ray duly arrived, just as loving as ever. During dinner, I said to him, "She was very pretty, wasn't she?"

"Who?"

"The blonde woman in the green dress you were sitting next to at the dinner on Saturday."

His jaw dropped.

"You were chatting her up, weren't you?"

"I was. She was lovely." I guess he thought it was a fair cop.

"What stopped you?"

"Well, the most peculiar thing happened. I really was very tempted by her, when suddenly a picture of you appeared before my eyes. It was so clear it was like a photograph and then I realised how much you meant to me. I just couldn't do that to you. But how on earth did you know?"

I shrugged nonchalantly and didn't reply. Some things are best left a mystery, but all the time we were together, he was much too frightened ever to stray again. Nice one, Gran!

CHAPTER 7

After John died, I needed a project and decided to remodel my house. I spent so long knocking the guts out of it that the builders became like family. They were a lovely crew. During one of the numerous tea breaks, the conversation turned to jobs they had worked on before. The plumber was a no-nonsense South London chap called Rob who had, for a while, worked at the Tower of London. The plumbing work had to be done at night so as not to disturb the tourists, and when he first started the job, he had no qualms about working the night shift. However, gradually his views changed. He said that although he had never actually seen anything, he had been so conscious of someone or something watching him that he had had to leave what was a very lucrative job.

The manager of the building crew was Don, a good-looking Jack the Lad of immense charm with a constant twinkle in his eye and a great Cockney sense of humour. One evening he rang me.

"Hi, babe. I just wanted to let you know I won't be in tomorrow."

"What's wrong? Are you ill?"

"No, I'm doing a runner. I haven't told anyone else, but you've been good to me and I didn't want to let you down."

"But, Don, why? Are you in some sort of trouble?"

"No, but I've got this bird, see. I'm leaving the old trouble and strife (wife) and going off with Michelle."

I made the appropriate noises, said we would miss him, but hoped he would be happy.

A few days later, he rang again.

"Hi, Suze. It's Don. I've told Michelle all about you and she wants to meet you. Can I bring her over to see you?"

"Of course. I'd love to meet her."

I was slightly bemused because, at that time, I didn't know Don all that well, and besides, I couldn't imagine what he could possibly have told Michelle that would make her so keen to meet me.

We agreed a time for them to pop in for a drink. At the appointed hour, Don arrived with a stunningly beautiful girl. She was tall and slender with long blonde hair and huge blue eyes. I could quite understand why Don had "done a runner".

We chatted stiffly at first as Michelle seemed quite shy, but then Don said, "I've told her all about you and the ghosts." This opened the floodgates. Michelle started to talk nineteen to the dozen. It transpired she had been seeing 'people' from when she was a very small girl and she was desperate to share her experiences with someone who could understand. We swapped tales of sightings for a while and then she told me a fascinating story.

She had two little girls and she had taken them to Hampton Court for a day out. It was in the autumn and getting dusk as the Palace was closing. She eventually managed to round up the girls and herded them towards the way out. As they got to the exit, the security guard started to close the door after them.

"Hang on," said Michelle. "There's still someone in there."

"No, you're the last," said the security guard.

"You're wrong. There is someone still on that last staircase. She was just behind us."

There was a pause. By now a second guard had come over and they conferred together for a moment.

"Would you mind coming with us, Madam?" said one of the guards.

Now, Michelle panicked. She was on the periphery of one of the well-known South London 'families' and was no stranger to the forces of law and order, having herself been charged a few times with petty crimes and misdemeanours. Hearing those words brought a chill, especially as, this time, she knew she was completely innocent.

"What for? I haven't done anything," she retorted, eyeing the girls balefully to see if they had nicked some bit of English Heritage while she wasn't looking.

"It's quite alright, Madam. There's nothing wrong, but we would be grateful if you would come with us," said the guard.

She was taken into an office where a man sat behind a desk. "Thank you for coming," he said. "Please, have a seat."

Michelle sat down, looking suspiciously around. The man produced a large ledger and opened it.

"Now," he continued. "Could you tell me exactly what you saw on the stairs?"

The ledger contained a record of all the sightings that have occurred at Hampton Court over I don't know how many years.

I have no proof as to the veracity of this story, but it's a lovely thought. Some scribe writing "Lady from Croydon bumped into Anne Boleyn" or "Catherine Howard's been screaming in that corridor again," is a thought to be treasured.

You really expect to have some sort of supernatural experience in a place like the Tower of London or Hampton Court, in fact, it's practically obligatory, and you feel a slight frisson of disappointment if you come away without having had any form of spectral encounter, even if it's only a ghostly chill.

People say to me, "If I saw a ghost, I'd die of fright," but I always tell them spirits are not to be feared and, anyway, they probably wouldn't know at the time that it was indeed a spirit. It is generally only after the event you realise all was not as it seemed.

I do not usually see spirits, I feel them. I can describe them to you, tell you what they're saying, even tell you what they're wearing, but I do not see them as I see people.

When I was living in Wimbledon, I used to walk my aged Golden Retriever on the Common every afternoon. We would do a tour of the pond, or in Monty's case, a tour through the pond, and back up the cinder horse track. As Mont got older he would lag behind and I was constantly turning back to jolly him along.

One day, post pond, I turned to call him and saw a man walking behind me. He was very oddly dressed in plus fours, a mustard-coloured tweedy jacket, and an open neck shirt with a cravat. His sandy-coloured hair was parted in the middle and neatly Brylcreemed to either side, rather like the master of ceremonies in an Edwardian Music Hall, and around his neck hung a pair of opera glasses.

I started to feel uneasy. Not long before, a poor girl called Rachel Nickell had been brutally murdered on Wimbledon Common in broad daylight in front of her two-year son. The killer still hadn't been found. Naturally, the locals were all a bit twitchy, and here I was, all alone with a weirdo in a deserted part of the Common.

I grabbed Mont and put his lead on, but by this time he was tiring and his pace was slow. I was getting a bit panicky when, from a side path, emerged a gorgeous man. He was tall with chiselled features and polished ebony skin, and was clad in nothing but red satin running shorts and running shoes. I threw myself at him like a long lost friend.

"Hi! How are you? Lovely to see you again!"

The poor man looked terrified!

"I'm so sorry," I whispered. "But that man is following me."

As we turned to look, the strange man sloped off into the bushes.

"Are you alright, love?" asked my rescuer. "Shall I see you off the Common?"

"No, I'm fine now, thanks," I replied.

For all I knew, he could be a rapist or a mass murderer, so, tugging old Monty behind me, I hurried back to the car.

The next day, my friend Geoffie came for a walk with us. As I recounted the tale of my strange stalker, he became more and more worried.

"You know, you should vary your routine. It's not at all safe to walk the same route at the same time every day."

I thought about this for a moment as we walked along the horse track, our feet crunching on the cinders. I suddenly stopped dead.

"Oh my God! There was only the sound of one lot of footsteps yesterday. He was completely silent." I pondered a while longer. "That's okay then," I said. "I can cope with a ghostly Edwardian bird watcher."

Although the spirit world is usually very helpful, it's not all beer and skittles, and there are times when I would have preferred a little less spectral intervention.

Once the remodelling of my house was complete, I began to miss the cheery company of the builders and so, fired up by the compliments which had greeted the renovation of my own home, the idea came to me that I could do up houses and sell them on. I formed a property company, got a tame architect and, in my innocence and accompanied by my builder, Dave, went to see the bank manager, armed with sales details and plans for my project. I explained what I wanted to do and that I wanted to borrow some money to do it. The bank manager looked at my projections. "This seems like a good idea," he said. "Now tell me, how much do you want the bank to lend you?"

I regarded him in amazement. "Don't be silly, Mr. James. The lot, of course!"

There was a slight pause and then, blow me down, he agreed to a hundred percent loan! Dave nearly passed out.

They do say that God looks after fools and drunks. I don't know which I was, but he certainly looked after me, and I had a minor amount of success as a property developer. By this time, I also had a tame real estate agent called Ricky who would tip me off about promising properties.

One day, as I was cleaning out the attic, covered in dust and cobwebs, Ricky rang me.

"Get yourself down to Putney now. There's a house that's perfect for you. I'll hold it for a couple of hours before I let any other developers know."

"Okay," I said. "I'll meet you there in thirty minutes."

Half an hour later, still covered in dust and cobwebs, I drew up outside a large, attractive house. Ricky got out of his car and we went up the path together. He got out the keys, opened the front door and went in. The most awful chill enveloped me. "Good God!" I exclaimed. "What the hell happened here?"

"Dunno," replied Ricky shiftily. "Anyway, Dave will be here in a minute. I'll see you later."

He made to skedaddle out of the door.

"Oh, no you don't!" I said in alarm. "You'll stay here until Dave turns up. You're not leaving me here on my own."

A few minutes later, Dave arrived. Ricky made good his escape and Dave and I explored the property. It had once been a lovely house, but had been converted into rather crummy bedsits. We discovered a treasure trove of beautiful old Victorian fireplaces, cornicing, and ceiling roses that obviously had not come from the local DIY store. At the front of the house was an elegant hexagonal room, and at the back a huge salon that had more than likely been the old drawing room, with French windows opening onto an unkempt but sizeable garden. Just outside these glass doors was a large uneven patch of newly laid concrete.

Dave and I discussed the possible number of flats we could create, and how much work would be involved. It suddenly came to me that our profit margin would be more or less the same if we returned the house to its former glory and sold it as a single house. The sums seemed to make sense and we started work.

The house was built on three floors, but between the first and second floor was a half landing with a door leading to an attic space. The temperature always seemed to drop about six degrees on this landing.

Don had, by this time, left the divine Michelle and gone back to the old trouble and strife, and was again manager on this job. One day, for some unknown reason, we were poking round in the loft, tapping on walls – as you do – when we discovered one was hollow. I told the guys to go ahead and knock it down.

The next day, Don rang me.

"I knew that loft had to be bigger, Suze," he said. "The dimensions didn't add up. Now that we've demolished the wall, the room is half as big again."

This is always music to the ears of a property developer!

Work continued apace and the house started to rise again like a Phoenix from the ashes. Unfortunately, before it was completely finished, thanks to a friend who had a building company, I found out that Dave had been ripping me off dreadfully, and I had been paying him three times as much as I should have been. There was a parting of the ways, but not before Dave and his cronies caused quite some damage in a fit of pique.

Don remained faithful to me, along with a painter called Ron who had worked for me for donkey's years. It was Don who warned me about the damage and suggested I take photos in case we had to go to court.

It was now the end of August. As I was already in Putney to buy a tropical fish tank for Lulu's birthday, I decided to pop in to the house on my way home. It must have been about 6.30p.m. when I arrived, and the light was beginning to fade slightly. I had just let myself in and started to take pictures of the crime scene, when I began to get very cold and jittery. Not long before this, a young real estate agent called Susie Lamplugh had gone to meet a client referred to her in her appointment book as Mr. Kipper. The poor girl had totally disappeared, presumed murdered, and the client had also vanished into thin air. As I went round the house, I was convinced someone was watching me and kept glancing over my shoulder, but far from thinking about ghosts, I was afraid that maybe Mr. Kipper was lurking in the lengthening shadows. I got out of there tout de suite, trembling, but once I got into the car and turned on the radio to be greeted by the soothing strains of *The Archers*, I began to feel better.

The next morning, Don rang me.

"Hi, doll. How are you?"

"I'm fine thank you. I got the photos. I went and took them yesterday evening."

"Christ, Suze! You didn't go there on your own, did you?"

"Yes," I answered, puzzled. "Why ever not?"

"None of us would be there alone. We always waited for someone else to turn up before we went in."

"Why?"

Now, these were all big, burly lads who had never run from a spot of bother. "It was 'orrible. Definitely something nasty there."

"It was rather creepy," I whispered.

Between the two of them, Don and Ron finished the house and I sold it. We decided not to touch the garden and left it as it was, complete with the new patch of concrete which Ricky had explained away as the previous owner's attempt to lay a patio. I hadn't realised at the time, but dear old Ron had been staying late every evening to finish the decorating for me. He was a very down to earth, phlegmatic character and made no bones about his negative opinion of my belief in the supernatural. However, once the house was sold, he told me he was always scared on the half landing and on the second floor. Without my saying anything, he too had thought he was being watched – and that from a man who had always held that there were no such things as ghosts.

When I moved house, Don was doing some work for me at home. We started chatting about the Putney house.

"I've had nothing but bad luck since then," he said. He had been going through a particularly difficult time. "I think it's all down to the pen."

"What pen?"

"The young gal's pen." "What young girl?"

"The one whose case we found."

By now, this was getting a bit like twenty questions.

"You remember we knocked that wall down in the attic? Well, behind the wall we found a suitcase full of a young woman's stuff – clothes, makeup, passport, cheque book, credit cards, driver's licence and a bit of money."

"What?" This was the first I had heard of any suitcase. "What did you do with it?" I asked.

"We took the good stuff; cash, credit cards, things we could sell, and then threw the case on the skip."

I was absolutely horrified. No young girl would walk away from all her belongings like that, and who would go to the trouble of wiping out all traces of her existence, walling up her suitcase, and more importantly, why? There was something very peculiar and sinister going on here. My obvious first reaction was to go to the police, but I had no evidence and I knew none of the slightly fly-by-night builders would back me up.

"Do you remember the name on the documents?" I asked. "No," replied Don. "I just had this pen."

A while later, Don was again doing some work for me when a friend popped in. Over a cup of coffee, Don and I regaled her with the story, complete with gestures and dramatic pauses.

"But," asked my friend, "if someone had murdered a girl, what did they do with the body?"

Don and I looked at each other. Why hadn't we thought of it before?

"She's under the concrete!" we said, as one.

This house was my swan song as a property developer and I had moved on to other things. A couple of years after I sold it, I bumped into Ricky, the real estate agent.

"Hello," he said. "I haven't seen you for ages."

We got chatting and I explained I was no longer working in property.

"Do you remember that house we did?" I asked him. "I wonder how the new owners are getting on there."

"Funny you should say that. They didn't stay there long, only a few months. They sold at quite a reasonable price too. They seemed very keen on a quick sale. Actually, it's changed hands a couple of times since then. I don't know why it comes on the market so often. It's such a lovely house."

I didn't say a word!

CHAPTER 8

Property developing having run its course, I cast my mind around for something else to keep me occupied and out of mischief, and came to the conclusion that a language might be fun. I had done A-Level French and at one time I was reasonably fluent in Italian, thanks to summers spent at a pretty little town called Diano Marina on the Ligurian coast. I hummed and hawed between the two languages because, although my heart is Italian, I had a much more conventional and thorough grounding in French, thanks to Miss Syvret, a gorgon of a French teacher who scared the socks off me in the Lower Sixth.

Having made my choice, I rang my cousin Richard. He is a brilliant linguist and, at the last count, spoke about six languages fluently.

"What was that French exam you did at college?" I asked him.

"Institute of Linguists Intermediate. I did both French and German."

I later realised how impressive it was to do both at once, but then he is extremely bright.

"Do you think I could I do it?"

"Don't see why not," came the slightly dubious reply.

Having a young daughter to look after, I didn't fancy a university course, so I looked around for a private teacher. I found a delightful lady from Luxembourg called Sam, and made a start on my linguistic odyssey. For one so blonde and pretty and charming, Sam could, at times, have made Miss Syvret look like a pussycat, but she got results. I sat, and duly passed the Intermediate exam, but by this time I'd got the learning bug and decided to go for the Advanced. Everyone thought this a very ambitious goal as it is a higher qualification than a university degree, but I was determined. The workload was heavy but Sam cracked the whip and somehow I completed the course for the Finals.

It was at this time I realised that it was not only Gran and John helping me from the spirit world. During one of the sittings with Stephen, he had told me a Frenchman was with me.

"Don't know any French men," I mused. "Unless you count the barman at the Hotel Versailles."

"No, no. He was a diplomat at the court of Vienna during the Austro-Hungarian Empire."

"That's nice."

"I'm sure you knew him in a previous life. In fact, you might have been married to him. He's very handsome."

Damn! Pity I couldn't remember him!

"Anyway," continued Stephen, "he's here to help you and give you support."

I had half-forgotten this until I did my Final Diploma. I have always been scared of exams, although I usually do quite well in them. I'm one of those people who mug everything up at the last minute, reproduce the knowledge in the exam, and then promptly forget about it. However, until the adrenaline kicks in, I'm a gibbering wreck.

The finals were held at the Polish Centre in Hammersmith, and lasted five days. As parking was/is such a bugger in that area, my lovely Don offered to act as chauffeur. I sat in his car the first morning, shaking and muttering to myself. We got to the Centre. I got out of the car and started to climb the steps. Then the most peculiar thing happened. Although my feet were firmly on the ground, I felt as if someone had taken me by the elbows and lifted me a couple of inches off the floor. My nerves disappeared.

The first exam was the Long Essay. We had had to prepare and submit in advance the titles of six two thousand word essays within a chosen category. I had chosen Politics and Recent History, and there was one essay in particular on the Rise of the French Socialist Party of which I was particularly proud. I floated into the hall and found my desk. As I turned over the exam paper, my heart leapt. I had got the subject I'd hoped for. I took up my pen and suddenly, as if on a screen, the essay Sam and I had honed to perfection appeared before my eyes. I started to scribble. The exam was due to last three hours, but I was done in one and a half. I checked it carefully, got up, placed my finished paper on the invigilator's desk and left, accompanied by pitying glances from my fellow students who obviously thought it had all been too much for me.

That afternoon was the Oral, my absolute least favourite. Again, we had had to prepare and submit five ten minute talks to be chosen on the spot by the examiner. Now, although it was against the rules, I had learnt all five off by heart. The examiner was charming and quickly put me at my ease.

"Please speak to me about 'Le Culte du Corps'," he said. Again, this was my favourite – a slightly ambitious, but I hoped amusing, spoof on the body fixation of the early eighties. Again, the scroll appeared before my eyes. I spoke for a few minutes. The examiner must have twigged that I had learned this by rote and interrupted me with a question, obviously designed to break my train of thought. The autocue paused. I smiled sweetly and answered his question. The autocue started to roll again and I carried on.

Every day, as I walked up the steps of the Polish Centre, I felt myself lifted, and I can honestly say that I have never written or spoken such good French before or since. I am convinced to this day that I had some sort of divine help. I must have been a good wife all those years ago!

I passed the exam and went on to become a Member of the Institute of Linguists, an achievement of which I am inordinately proud. I must say, it gave me great pleasure to ring Cousin Richard to gloat that I am better qualified than he is, even though we both know his French is streets ahead of mine as he is virtually bilingual. In fact, the only time I have dared to speak French in front of him was at my sixtieth birthday party, fuelled by a couple of glasses of champagne and faced with a guest who didn't speak English.

However, although very qualified from the language point of view, I didn't have a teaching diploma which precluded me from teaching in a school. I decided to become a tutor, which turned out to be a great decision as I earned more money for less time, and also got to teach a vastly diverse range of people. I taught adult beginners and Common Entrance, O-Level, A-Level, and my favourite, a hugely intelligent post graduate who only wanted to do very high-level translations.

My first pupil was a twelve-year-old boy who rejoiced in the name of Daenson Rodwell Scipio, a name which could surely have only presaged great things. He was such a bright boy, and a joy to teach. His family was from Guyana and, in typical Caribbean style, his granny used to go to church every Sunday, resplendent in a straw hat bedecked with flowers. One day there was tragic news. Granny's mum had been killed. She had been walking to market when a car had skittled her. Everybody was in shock. They had not been expecting news of her death as she was only ninety. I wrote Granny a note to say how sorry I was for her loss, and after that I was taken into the bosom of the family.

Daenson's mum used to ring me to ask my advice about everything under the sun, ranging from extremely personal problems to what wall paper she should choose. In fact, as a friend remarked, if the phone rang late Saturday afternoon, it was bound to be either Daenson's mother, or the butcher, drunk as a skunk, calling to make sure my latest boyfriend was treating me properly!

I especially loved teaching Common Entrance. There is something very endearing about eleven-year-old boys struggling with the mysteries of another language when they seem often to be having difficulties with their mother tongue. One sock up, one sock down and tie somewhere under an ear.

Common Entrance was a doddle. I had a list of questions and the kids learnt the answers like little parrots. One of my boys, Tom, was struggling with a written comprehension.

"Le 14 juillet, feux d'artifice à la place."

"Let's break this down," I said encouragingly. "What is le 14 juillet?"

"14th July. Bastille Day."

"Great. And 'à la place'?"

"In the main square."

"Fantastic. So what do you think feux d'artifice means, bearing in mind that we have Bastille Day celebrations in the main square?"

Total blank!

"Okay. What does 'feux' mean?"

"Fires."

"Super! And d'artifice?"

"Um." He screwed his eyes up as if in dreadful pain. He pulled his tie so far around his neck, I thought for an awful moment that he was trying to hang himself! "Artificial?"

Now we were getting somewhere.

"Excellent! So we have artificial fires in the main square on 14th July. Come on, Tom. You can do this!"

Surely by now he'd realised it meant fireworks.

The pained expression that always accompanied the thought process faded and a beam of comprehension began to dawn.

"Gas fires!" he exclaimed proudly.

I think my favourite pupil was Harry, a freckle-faced young lad with bright red hair and Harry Potter glasses, whose passion in life was fishing. He would go out with his father every weekend and loved to tell me what he had caught. He was a straight A student in all subjects except French, in which he committed the cardinal sin of getting a B! His mother was a rather unpleasant and pushy woman, and was determined to improve his grade. Harry was a joy to teach, but determined to sidetrack me at every given opportunity. As we were ploughing through the pitfalls of the preceding direct object, Harry said, "Just been to Australia."

"I know. Was it good?"

"Great. Was in the earthquake."

There had just been a medium sized tremor Down Under. "Oh, Harry! Was it scary?" I asked.

"Naw! Not scared at all."

We carried on with the lesson. A few minutes later, he said, "Went diving on the Great Barrier Reef."

Small boys seem unable to use many pronouns. "That must have been wonderful."

"Saw a shark while I was swimming."

"God, you must have been terrified!" I said, knowing that if saw a shark up close and personal, I would die of fright.

"Naw! Nothing to it!"

"Gosh, Harry. You are brave."

Harry sat up tall and straightened his tie. "Do you like fish?" he asked.

Quite a non sequitur, but I guess we had been talking about sharks. "Very much," I replied.

"Well, don't be surprised to find one on your doorstep one day."

A couple of days later, his mother rang. "I have something for you," she said rather frostily. "Can I pop round?"

A few minutes later I opened the door to see her holding a beautiful large brown trout. "Harry caught this especially for you," she sniffed. "I can't think why!"

It seems even twelve-year-old boys are susceptible to a bit of flattery.

When I first started teaching, I decided to put an advertisement in the local newspaper. I knew that it was not a good idea to put "French lessons given. Ring Suzi," but thought that "French coaching to A-Level by Member of the Institute of Linguists" had a rather nice ring to it. Oh dear! I did get some strange phone calls and had to put quite a few men straight on what it was that I was offering!

One evening, the phone rang. I picked it up.

"Hello," said an educated-sounding male voice. "I'm enquiring about French lessons."

"Do you want proper French lessons or do you want a hooker?" I snapped, having got a bit fed up with randy ringers.

"Oh dear," stammered the caller. "Um, French lessons. Er, I'm going to spend a couple of months in France."

I apologised and explained, and we made an appointment for him to come round. And so Geoffie came into my life. He was kind to me at a time when I needed a bit of emotional gentleness, and he made me laugh. Unfortunately, he was a very expensive luxury, and not the slightest bit backward in letting me pay for everything.

He had resigned from his job as a middle-ranking civil servant to go on a quest. He was going to France to count tortoises! He spoke reasonable French and, after a few lessons, was more than capable of managing to count carapaces. He duly set off across the Channel to find his tortoises, and also to find the straw wine of the Jura, which he assured me was total nectar. He arrived back with half a bottle of the stuff because he was too mean to buy a whole one, and opened it with great ceremony. I don't know if he had got a bottle that was corked, or if the poor wine had suffered too much from being carried around next to Geoffie's sweaty socks, but it was disgusting!

While he was in France, he sent me love letters in French, which I corrected in red pen and sent back to him. This rather set the tone for our relationship.

I had once been told that when I was in my forties I would be doing two jobs at once. This certainly proved true, as it was about this time that I also became a clairvoyant. Since the débâcle of my first two readings, I had fought shy of psychic work. I had done readings for friends, or come out with spur of the moment predictions, but had not sought any kind of professional engagements.

At that time I worked with hands, not as a palmist, but by using the contact as a channel. Then Lulu bought me some exquisite Tarot cards for my birthday. I didn't have a clue what to do with them and kept meaning to read a book to find out, but somehow never got round to it. Little Sue, who was an incredibly gifted Tarot reader, came to see me.

"What fantastic cards," she said, picking them up and looking at them admiringly. "I've never seen any like these before. Why aren't you using them?"

"I don't know how to," I replied. "I don't even know how to lay out a spread."

"It doesn't matter. Just put them down anyhow and say what you see."

And so it was that I started my work as a psychic. I'm a little hazy about how I began to get known, but people started ringing me for readings. I do believe that, when the time is right, spirit will hold out a hand and it is up to you if you take it. This was my time to take that hand.

My clientèle grew rapidly, and it did come to pass that I was doing two jobs at the same time. The trouble was when the two overlapped. I would just say here that it is very important to close down after a reading. I was quite bad at remembering to do this until I learnt a very salutary lesson.

I had been asked to coach a young American lad for an Ivy League entrance exam. I explained to his parents that I had absolutely no knowledge of either the standard or the format, but they got hold of some previous exam papers and off we went. It was both interesting and challenging. Chris was a very bright young man and a pleasure to teach. The only fly in the ointment was his timekeeping, which was fluid to say the least. He could, and frequently did, turn up a good hour either side of the appointed time.

One day I had booked a reading, leaving what I thought was more than enough time before Chris' lesson to accommodate even his strange idea of punctuality. Three-quarters of an hour before he was due, Chris arrived. To tell the truth, I was a bit miffed with him and so I settled him down with some extra hard work and went back to my client. When we finished the reading, I went straight on to the lesson without taking a break. As it progressed, I started to feel really ill. I had a sore throat, my head was throbbing, and I felt very weak and faint. I couldn't think what was wrong until it dawned on me that Chris was off school with glandular fever. I was picking up his symptoms! I excused myself and went to close down before resuming the lesson, but I must say I was a bit easier on the poor lad after that.

CHAPTER 9

If ever a psychiatrist tried to analyse my dreams, I'm sure he would end up slightly barmy himself. I dream every night, some good, some bad, but always rambling, confused dreams which I'm sure means that I have a rambling, confused personality.

I have a very good friend called Belinda. She is tiny, but used to be a professional tennis player and was highly ranked in her day. She is no slouch on a tennis court, and it always amazes me that someone with such small hands can even hold a racket, let alone whack hell out of a ball like she does. When I met her, she had given up the circuit and was head of relocation with a very well-known merchant bank.

The first time she came to me for a reading, I saw a very different future ahead for her.

"You are going to do something spiritual," I said. "It's a very old art and something to do with Japan."

"Bloody hell!" came the reply. Nothing could have been further from her current job.

We soon became firm friends and partners in crime, and gradually, Belinda found herself becoming very drawn to Reiki at a time when this was an unknown quantity. In the right hands it is an extremely powerful healing process, and I strongly believe it should, like a lot of similar practices, only be carried out by qualified practitioners. Belinda has great healing powers and eventually gave up her high-powered job to become a full-time Reiki healer. She now works with horses and is a horse whisperer par excellence.

Anyway, Belinda used to have psychic dreams. She kept a book by the bed in which she wrote them down. The information that the spirit world gave to her proved to be amazingly accurate and very useful.

I don't know what spirit is trying to tell me. I dream that I'm walking down the street clad in nothing but a little short vest; a garment I have not worn since I was twelve and got my first bra. I dream that I'm shopping in Harrods, or some such posh store, wearing my ratty old dressing gown. I still dream that I have only one week to go before A-Levels and I haven't even started my revision – what the heck does that mean forty years on? Or that I'm due to leave for the airport in five minutes and haven't even started to pack.

The most common dream I have is that I have fifty people coming for dinner and only one small leg of lamb to feed them. Hint to husband: must mean I cook too much and need to go out to dinner more!

The best dream I have is that I can fly. I just hop off the ground like a fat pheasant and start to swim in the air. That is a lovely one and I'm always sorry to wake up. Why is it that when you have a nightmare it's often hard to come out of it, whereas if you dream that Gregory Peck in his handsome prime is making mad, passionate love to you, you wake immediately? I cannot count the number of times I have lain in bed, eyes tight shut, willing myself back into those manly arms while Gregory fades gently into the distance.

They do say that you never dream about the moment of your death. You can have a dreadful nightmare that you are about to perish in a particularly gruesome fashion, but you always wake up in a muck-sweat just before the actual occurrence. However, my brother-in-law dreamt he was going to be hanged. He ascended the gallows. The preacher gave him the last rites. They placed the hood over his head. The hangman's hand reached for the lever. Now, this is the time when most of us would have woken up screaming. Not Michael. He actually felt the noose tighten and felt himself falling through the trap door. He said he knew he was dead, but this didn't seem to worry him at all. But then, he always was a rather peculiar chap.

But there are some dreams that, even to me, seem different. For about three or four years, I had a dream that I was in a house or a flat overlooking the ocean. The actual building could change, but the huge expanse of glass overlooking a sandy beach and an azure sea beyond remained constant. Suddenly, I would see a great wall of water coming towards me. Just as the towering wave broke against the window, I would wake up, so I don't know whether I would have survived. Lulu and I were talking about dreams a while ago, and I was telling her about this. "Funny," I said. "I haven't had that dream for a long time now."

"That's odd," replied Lulu. "I regularly used to have a dream a bit like that, but I was standing on a beach and the sea literally disappeared before coming back as a gigantic wave. But now you mention it, I haven't had it for a good few years." She paused thoughtfully. "In, fact, not since the tsunami."

Had we both seen this tragically terrifying event in our dreams? After all, Mrs. Caesar had foreseen Lockerbie.

Another dream was that I was in a fantastic house, like a set from House and Garden. It was painted cool white with clean-lined white furniture, relieved by the odd piece of black lacquer or splashes of vibrant colour; something very avant-garde for its day when most of us were still floundering in a sea of chintz. There was a magnificent conservatory or orangery, full of huge palms and ferns, and in the centre was a very old, very large stone table with grooves channelled along all four sides. In my dream, it seemed to me that this table had its origins in an ancient world.

One evening, my friend Allie – she of the funny little Cheshire Cat man in Ealing – started to tell me about a vivid dream she'd had about a beautiful white house with a conservatory and a huge stone table with grooves down the sides. I looked at her in amazement. She'd pinched my dream!

Not long after this, she rang me to say she'd got a new boyfriend. She was very excited about him and was quite smitten. He was about twenty years older than she was, but gorgeous.

"What's his name?" I asked.

"J.T." she replied, mentioning the name of a man who had been notorious in the sixties for his underworld connections and amazingly impressive tackle.

"Not *the* J.T.?" I asked.

"I don't know. What are you talking about?"

Allie, being ten years younger than me, had never heard of him.

"Be careful," I warned. "If it's the same guy, you're playing with fire."

"Silly old cow," my friend said sweetly. "Don't worry, he's a pussycat."

A few days later the phone rang. "It's me," hissed Allie.

"Where are you?"

"Behind a palm tree." "What palm tree?"

"It's in the house."

"What house?"

"The one in our dream. The one with the table. It's a fab table but has these strange grooves down the sides. It's ever so old. Looks like it's come out of a museum. Oops! Got to go," and with that, Secret Squirrel hung up.

Suddenly my blood ran cold. I could see the table in my mind's eye, but this time it was covered in gore. The grooves were runnels for the blood. I thought to myself, "A life will be sacrificed." It did cross my mind that I was being a tad dramatic, but I was worried.

Things don't appear that clearly without a reason. I tried to ring Allie back, but she had turned off her phone.

The next morning, she rang me. "Are you alright?" I asked.

"Alright? I'll say! Had a fabulous night. What a guy! Best I've ever had!"

Obviously the rumours about his tackle had been correct.

My fears started to ease, but a few weeks later, Allie rang me to tell me she was pregnant. J.T. was the father but he didn't want to know, and dropped her like a hot potato. In her situation there was only one option for her, and that was an abortion. Whereas I would not go so far as to say that I don't believe in abortion under any circumstances, I feel the rules need tightening up. I know a few women who have had them and, without fail, it comes back to haunt them as they get older.

Allie was desolate. She loved kids and was great with them, but at that time it would have been impossible for her to cope. She felt bereft and guilty, and said to me, "You know, Suze, I sacrificed that child for my own selfish ends."

The image of the table sprang into my mind. That was the life that had been sacrificed.

I had another experience of a shared dream. My relationship with husband John was not always an easy one and during the five years he was sick, his personality underwent quite an aggressive change, due in no small measure to the cocktail of drugs he had to take. After his death, the sadness was tinged a little with relief that I didn't have to spend so much time in hospitals, and that I could give my little girl the attention she so rightly deserved. My small world seemed to have settled down rather nicely, and my social life had picked up no end. But then the dream started.

I was in a cheerful house filled with bright colours and light. The sun would be shining, I would be pottering about, happy and contented with my life, when the doorbell would ring. I would open it to find John on the doorstep.

"Hello, darling," he would say. "Isn't it wonderful? They made a mistake. I'm not dead after all."

"Wonderful," I would reply faintly. "That's fantastic." All the time my heart was heavy, thinking I was about to lose my comfy life.

Now, I know this can be explained away and put down to all sorts of feelings that surface after a loved one dies, but there is a twist.

Best friend, Joy, is no good at keeping things to herself. You can trust her to take any secret of yours to the grave, but when it comes to her own feelings, she's totally transparent. She popped in to see me one day, looking decidedly hot and bothered. "What's wrong, Joyous?"

"Nothing," she lied, plonking herself down in the kitchen and lighting a cigarette. I fixed her with a stony stare. "I can't tell you."

I continued my Gorgon impression. She squirmed and took a huge drag on the cigarette.

"Well, I had this really weird dream. You and Sarah (my other best friend) and I were in the South of France."

This sounded good.

"We were on a beach and I decided to go ahead to the beach restaurant and book a table for lunch."

Even better!

"When I got there, I found that John was in charge. He came up and said hello to me, and I just blurted out, 'But you're dead!' 'It's been a mistake,' he replied, 'but don't tell Suzi. I want to surprise her.' I didn't know how to warn you. You and Sarah looked so happy walking along the beach together, laughing."

It was a variation on my dream.

CHAPTER 10

People often ask me if I believe in reincarnation. The answer is that I'm almost sure I do. It is, after all, an explanation of genius. Knowledge accumulated over past lives could explain Mozart composing symphonies at three, or polymaths like Leonardo da Vinci.

I have also read some very impressive studies undertaken in India, where children in Goa, for example, can describe lives and people in the Punjab or Nepal. When these stories have been investigated, it has been found that the details of these other lives can be corroborated, and often they relate to families who had lost a child just before the child from Goa was born.

If pressed for an opinion, I think I would have to say that some people are reincarnated and some stay in the spirit world, but I do pity God having to decide who stays, who goes, and where they go. Can't be all beer and skittles being the Almighty!

My cousin, for reasons best known to her, decided to be regressed - that is taken back to previous lives under hypnosis. I don't know why she felt the need, and as she is a very strong practising Catholic, I had the niggling feeling that she could be committing some sort of sin. Nevertheless, she seemed to find it the panacea for all ills.

I must admit that I was curious, and I went to see the lady hypnotist/ psychic in the genteel Surrey town of Haslemere.

Before we started the session, she got me to make two lists. One of things I really liked, and one of things that I hated or that scared me. Prominent on the list of fears were dark, confined spaces, moths and butterflies or anything fluttering, and decapitation.

I didn't know which list to put Red Indians on. Every Saturday afternoon when I was a child, my father and I would go to the Vogue Cinema at Tooting Bec in South London to watch Cowboy and Indian films, and ever since that time, I have been totally obsessed. I do here and now apologise unreservedly to all the noble Native American nations who I hold in great respect, but in my mind they are something completely separate from the red devils of Saturday afternoon oaters!

I will watch any western, no matter how bad, and I must have seen *The Searchers* – the best Western ever - at least thirty times. In fact, I could probably understudy for any of the roles. I am completely fascinated by anything to do with the Apache or Comanche, but to me, one of the most terrifying experiences would have been to be under siege in a wagon or ranch in the early days of the West. In fact, for years as a child, when I went to bed, I would pull the covers right over my head so that - in the unlikely event that Geronimo or Cochise made it to South West London and crawled in through my bedroom window - they wouldn't see me under the blankets.

Anyway, down they went on both lists for luck. The hypnotist lady didn't look at these lists until after the session, which was recorded.

We started down the usual hypnosis route: relaxation, warmth, sunshine, sandy beach, waves lapping gently. Then she told me to imagine a book that was the book of my life, and to turn the pages back to myself at various ages. My voice on the recording becomes younger all the time. Eventually, she told me to turn back past my birth.

Now for the strange bit. I was on a hillside somewhere in Greece, or maybe what is now Turkey. It was just before dusk and I was with a handsome young man who was telling me how beautiful I was, and declaring his love for me. So far, great! Then the scene changed. I was in a dark cave, lying in a shallow hole. There was a board on my chest, upon which rocks were being placed by priests. It seemed that I was part of a very early Earth Mother cult, maybe even predating Troy, but I kept insisting that I had been chosen to serve "The God" not the goddess. The priests wore very distinctive hats, high-crowned rather like Greek Orthodox priests, but gold rather than black, and adorned with strange hieroglyphics. The words that kept coming to my mind were "Samarian" and "Aramaic" although this means nothing to me and I don't even know if there is a connection between the two.

The rocks became heavier and heavier. I was having trouble breathing. In the flickering light of the priests' torches I could see bats fluttering in the dark recesses of the cave. Suddenly, I felt as if I were in a vortex. I was being pulled upwards in a sort of conical whirlpool towards a pinprick of light. Gradually I became aware of someone calling my name, "Suzi! Suzi, come back! Breathe! For God's sake, breathe!"

At this point, the voice of the hypnotist on the tape sounds panic-stricken. The light and the vortex faded away and I began to breathe normally again.

The next life we explored was someone famous. I won't tell you who it was because so many people have been Napoleon, or Julius Caesar, or some other well-known person, that it makes me think that any ancient celebrity must have been suffering from multiple personality disorder. Suffice to say it was a woman who met an untimely end at the hands of an axe man.

The third and last life we visited was fascinating, but rather sad. I was a little girl living in America in the 19th Century. I think I must have been in Arizona because, in the distance, I could see one of those huge three-pronged cacti like you see in Snoopy cartoons, and I think they grow mainly in southern Arizona. On the tape you can hear a child's voice speaking with an American accent. It was my birthday and I was so proud of the new shoes that Daddy had gone into town to get for me. Mommy was going to bake a special cake and we were going to have a party, just me, Mommy, and Daddy. I was very excited.

The hypnotist told me to go forward a couple of days. I was standing on the porch looking at the cactus. I don't know why, because I couldn't see anything untoward, but I felt very scared. We pressed the regression fast forward button three days. The child's voice was now feeble. The hypnotist asked where I was.

"I'm in my special hiding place. Mommy made me go there to hide from the Indians. She told me to wait until she came for me, but she hasn't come. I'm so thirsty and I'm so sleepy."

"Go to the next day," said the hypnotist.

Nothing. It seems that I had just passed quietly away in my hiding place.

Could this, as well as the Vogue, Tooting, be responsible for my obsession with Red Indians? The famous lady could explain my fear of beheadings, and the fact that I had twice met my end in dark, confined spaces could explain my fear of the dark and my slight claustrophobia, as could the presence of the bats in that ancient cave explain the fear of all things fluttering. All in all, it was a fascinating experience.

There is a theory that if you are either very drawn to, or very scared of, a particular period in history, the chances are that you may have lived in it. In my case, I adore anything to do with Ancient Greece or Rome, am madly in love with Charles II, and totally hate anything to do with the Middle Ages.

I have had quite clear flashbacks to a time in Ancient Greece. Not the sacrificial one from the regression, but a much more civilised age. I had a comfortable life. My husband and I were not part of the Athenian or Spartan courts, but we were well off. We had an estate that produced olives and lemons, as well as wine, honey, and grain. It was on a plateau which rose as a steep scarp from the coastal plain, and you could see the sea shimmering in the distance. I was quite a tall, broad-shouldered woman with, surprisingly, I thought for a southern Mediterranean woman, beautiful thick blonde hair which was carefully coiffed and coiled. I wore a white robe with an unusual intricately plaited belt.

Now, I have a very dear friend called Bob who has helped me enormously over the years. He suffers from MS, but is one of the nicest, most uncomplaining men you could possibly meet, and I am in awe of his psychic abilities. One day, when we were chatting, he said to me, "You used to live in Ancient Greece."

He then went on to describe me as I had seen myself, even down to the intricate belt. "How do you know this?" I asked in astonishment.

"I was there too."

Around this time, my friend Patti's husband had a Malayan accountant called Nithy, who was also very psychic (handy type of accountant that!) and a great healer. He too helped me on my spiritual path and became a good friend. Amazingly, he also, without my having said a word, described the Ancient Greek Suzi.

"My God! You were there too," I exclaimed.

"Yes. I was a doctor."

This was too much. The three of us had known each other in a previous life. Nithy and Bob had never met, and I had long discussions with them individually as to whether the three of us should get together. The strange thing was, much as it was tempting, we never had the courage. I don't know what we thought would happen. Perhaps we would have uncovered some hidden wormhole that would whisk us back to Ancient Greece. Perhaps we would have unleashed a force better kept contained. Who knows? I just know that, even now, I feel a slight sense of relief that we didn't tempt fate.

CHAPTER 11

When Lulu was little, she decided she wanted to learn to play the piano. I was all for this, even having visions of taking it up again myself having struggled through a year's tuition from Miss Primrose Arabella Ivermee when I was at school.

Husband John had an Uncle Bert who was a fence, but hid his trade behind the respectable façade of a TV repair shop. Uncle Bert was married to Auntie Alice, a short, square, militant woman. When I first met them, I was very impressed that they had monogrammed silver cutlery ⊠ A & H R ⊠ Alice and Herbert Roper. How very posh, I thought, until I realised that every day Uncle Bert went for lunch to Arding & Hobbs Restaurant and every day nicked his place setting!

Uncle Bert was quite a character. When he started to go bald, he informed us all that as Brewer's Yeast was supposed to be good for hair loss, he would rub it into his thinning pate. We tried gently to point out that you were supposed to take it, but Bert would have none of this and continued to rub in the orange-coloured paste. Miraculously, it worked, and a thatch of new hair sprouted. However, it was slightly startling as it grew back bright ginger.

Alice and Bert hated each other, not helped by the fact that Bert had an elderly girlfriend called Mrs. Flynn.

By the time our wedding came round, tensions were running high. My family was bad enough, split between my father's genteel

Home Counties respectability and my mother's coal mining Yorkshire contingent, but add rather dubious connections to certain South London "families" on my future husband's side and you had a potent brew.

My mother had more than a touch of the Hyacinth Buckets about her. She was set on giving her only daughter a grand wedding and was determined that restricted funds and location (St Mary's, Balham) would not stop her. It was planned with military precision. John's father had very sadly died before I met him, so whereas Daddy would escort my future mother-in-law down the aisle, it left Mummy at a loose end. "Bertie shall escort me," she trilled.

The day dawned. Mummy was resplendent in cerise with fur trim. Uncle Bert sported his anorak, which went well with his shock of ginger hair. The photos bear witness that Mummy was not happy. However, she did manage a semblance of a smile through gritted teeth, and no incident occurred until we left the church where we found, as part of the congregation, Mrs. Flynn! Uncle Bert's black eye, the result of a swift left hook from Auntie Alice, provided a colourful contrast to the carrot hair.

Auntie Alice was an excellent cook, but always fed Bert with out of date Fray Bentos meat pies. He seemed to survive, in spite of the odd upset stomach, until he dropped down dead while mending the vicar's television. Nobody seemed that fussed about poor old Uncle Bert's departure, nevertheless, every evening at least a dozen assorted relations would cluster around Auntie Alice and go visit Uncle Bert in the funeral parlour. I had never come across this custom before, and had the rather sneaky feeling that they were going to make sure he was still there.

One day before his sad demise, Bert called us to say that he had found us a piano and asked if we could go and look at it. Off we trotted to a flat in Balham High Road where we met a delightful elderly couple. The piano – an extremely good but rather unattractive baby grand – had belonged to their son who, many years before had been killed while in the services. They had kept the piano but now found themselves fallen on hard times and forced to sell it. Having taken my father, the musician of the family, along to check it out – John and I having the musical ears of stoats on heat – we duly bought it and installed it in our dining room where it was played for a brief period until Lulu's interest waned and it served as a rather cumbersome stand for vases of flowers and photographs.

A few years after its installation, on a beautiful spring morning with the sun streaming through the windows, I went into the dining room carrying a vase of daffodils to be greeted by the sight of a young man seated at the piano. As I walked in he stood up, inclined his head slightly, and said, "Hello, I'm Christopher."

He was a somewhat foppish young man of about twenty-eight, with Hugh Grant hair, wearing an old-fashioned smoking jacket with quilted lapels.

Now, I didn't panic too much as I didn't think a mass murderer or burglar would take the trouble to introduce himself so politely, but it did cross my mind that maybe he was something to do with Atkinson Morley Psychiatric Unit which wasn't too far away. In fact, the lovely Joyous had once come across a man standing on a street corner, dressed in his pyjamas and carrying a standard lamp. Being an ex-nursing sister, she had immediately taken control of the situation, bundled him into the car and delivered him to Atkinson Morley where he had been welcomed back with open arms.

"Can I help you?" I asked the young man.

"No, thank you. I've just come to see my piano."

Definitely Atkinson Morley!

"Your piano?"

"Yes. Lovely, isn't it? Super tone. I say, it's awfully nice to meet you."

With that he got up and walked around the piano towards me and I realised he had no feet. There was just a sort of mist where they should have been.

Surprisingly, I wasn't scared and for some reason, I didn't even find it that bizarre. I just said it had been lovely but I had to get on. I rummaged through drawers until I found an antique packet of fags and by the time I'd puffed and choked my way through a couple, I'd convinced myself it was my imagination.

I hadn't banked on Christopher's penchant for performing. Periodically he would go into concert mode, which was quite delightful as he was a very accomplished pianist and rather partial to a bit of Grieg. Unfortunately, he didn't show himself on these occasions, as if the effort of materialising and playing at the same time was too much, but he did love an audience. Suddenly, usually towards the cheese course of a dinner party, the piano would take off like the automatic one that used to be in Harrods. You could hear the music and see the keys going up and down, but no maestro! As you can imagine, this used to unsettle the dinner guests somewhat, all the more when I explained there was no cause for concern – it was only the ghost. I did notice though, that the amount of alcohol consumed used to increase in direct ratio to the enthusiasm of Christopher's playing, and liqueurs were rarely refused.

In the same room was a rocking chair that had been in my Yorkshire family for about four generations. I had had it restored and it stood, rather malevolently, in a corner. No-one ever sat in it because it was uncomfortable and tucked away. Obviously someone liked it because it would start to rock on its own, often when Christopher was in full spate, and you could actually see grooves on the carpet that the rocking motion had worn down.

As I mentioned earlier, the piano wasn't terribly attractive and took up quite a lot of room, so I decided to sell it. I advertised it and had quite a few queries because it was a very well-respected make. But, whenever anyone came to see, anything they played sounded like Les Dawson, that wonderful comedian who would start playing beautifully and then hit all the wrong keys. It produced the most terrible out of tune racket and they would go away muttering about wasted journeys. The minute they had gone, the piano would revert to its original tone. I challenged Christopher on this. "I don't want to leave my piano."

"You won't have to leave your piano. You can go with it."

"I like it here."

It is extremely difficult to argue with a determined ghost.

In 1990 I met the man I would live with for the next six, turbulent years, very confusingly also called John. We met at a lunch party in the October, and two weeks later he took me to Rome for my birthday. On our second night there, he asked me to marry him. Swept off my feet by the suddenness of the proposal and carried away with an excess of Prosecco and Dolce Vita, I accepted. Luckily for me, the next morning he changed his mind, citing fear of commitment and the fact that he was still waiting for his decree nisi! At the time I was a bit miffed, but in retrospect it was the best thing that could have happened.

In fact, it was only marriage itself and the thought of another divorce settlement that scared him. He virtually moved in with me as soon as we got back to England and, not long after, we decided to buy a house together. In spite of the rather depressed housing market, I found a buyer for my house and decided that the piano definitely had to go. I made up my mind that even if I had to let it go cheaply to a dealer, I would cut my losses. The minute contracts were exchanged on the house, mould appeared all over the dining room walls. Horrible, smelly, black mould. Although rather surprised, I wasn't unduly concerned. I got the bleach out and washed it away. Now, bleach is supposed to kill mould spores, but the next day it was back. It didn't matter how many times I cleaned, I couldn't get rid of it for more than twenty-four hours.

The Sunday before I moved, I gave a drinks party to introduce the new people to the neighbours. I was talking to the new owner when Dermot, a wonderfully eccentric Irish barrister, came over and gave me a big hug.

"Sue, my darling girl. How are you? How's that ghost of yours?"

I nearly had a fit. Just a few weeks before there had been a case in America where a judge had ruled that a couple could get out of a house purchase contract because there was a ghost, and therefore the house didn't come with vacant possession. Nigel, the man buying the house, was also a barrister!

It was a perfect warm English summer's day, and the rather alcoholic but seemingly innocuous peach fizz was going down very well. Dermot, in an effort to change the subject, said, "Have you sold your piano yet?"

He was a very accomplished pianist and had managed to wrestle control of the keys from Christopher a few times, on one memorable occasion sporting a chapatti set at a rather rakish angle on his slightly balding head.

"No, not yet."

"How much do you want for it?"

"£x000"

"But that's a steal. It's worth much more than that."

By this time, thanks to the peach fizz, Nigel was swaying slightly in the breeze. "Er, I play the piano."

"Have you got one?" asked Dermot. "No."

"Well, you had better come with me immediately." Off they staggered.

Five minutes later Dermot returned, a huge grin on his face, brandishing a cheque for double the amount.

"Cash it quickly tomorrow before the hangover clears," he said gleefully.

The next morning, having scuttled to the bank at as soon as it opened at 9.30, I went into the dining room. The mould hadn't come back and Christopher was standing by the piano.

"Thank you. I'm happy now. I can stay here with my piano."

CHAPTER 12

There are times when foresight isn't really a great help.

The first Christmas John and I were together, I was determined to show off my skills as Domestic Goddess extraordinaire. I started to make plans for the festivities. Now, I am a total baby about Christmas. I absolutely love it. I adore the decorations and carols and last minute present buying, but most of all I love the cooking, and I spend many a happy hour up to my hips in flour and dried fruit. In fact, the only time this ever got stressful was when Lulu and our then lodger, Emma, decided to bath the guinea pig on the kitchen table whilst I was in the middle of baking a batch of mince pies.

My parents were coming for the holiday as usual, and John's mother and aunt were also coming. This would be our first meeting and so, naturally, I was extremely keen to impress.

About three weeks before Christmas, I began to get forebodings. I called the oven man.

"Would you come and look at my oven please?" "Certainly, madam. What's wrong with it?"

"Nothing."

"Er... if there's nothing wrong with it, why do you want me to look at it?"

"Because it's going to blow up on Christmas Eve."

The voice on the other end of the line became very calm and soothing.   I could imagine the notes he was making.

"Don't worry, madam. I'll be there tomorrow."

Sometimes the fact that I'm nicer to people who fix things for me than I am to the family pays off. I make them cups of tea and enquire about their families or ailments or, in the case of the washing machine man, his dog. He had an Afghan hound that was a better escapologist than Houdini, and his clients were always delivering it back to him. The dog would climb into any car and be driven happily home, head out of the window, tongue lolling, and ears flying in the slipstream.

Anyway, the next day the oven man duly arrived. I made him a cup of tea and he began a painstaking examination of the oven. After about an hour, he said to me, "There's absolutely nothing wrong. The oven is fine."

"Are you sure?"

"Completely. You don't have to worry."

Christmas Eve dawned brightly. My parents arrived, followed by John's mother and aunt, and other assorted bods we had collected along the way. John's mother was an adorable little lady called Poppy. She was the sweetest thing, but sadly had Alzheimer's, the same thing my mother was suffering from, although my mother wasn't quite so sweet. The two mothers hit it off famously, instantly becoming new best friends. They developed a rather curious pastime. In that house, the downstairs rooms were interconnecting. The two old ladies, handbags firmly clutched in both hands to their bosoms, spent their time shuffling sideways with a strange crab like gait, doing circuits of the ground floor and chatting nineteen to the dozen in a language unintelligible to the rest of us.

Aunt Margaret, on the other hand, was ninety-four and a cross between a Jack Russell and a Sherman tank. She and the Golden Retriever collided in the kitchen. We all held our breath while visions of *Casualty* danced in our heads – and the dog fell over!

At about 5 pm, having done most of the food preparation, I turned the oven on high and put the gleaming, clove studded ham into glaze.

There was an almighty bang and all the lights went out. I didn't panic because we had a dodgy iron that was always blowing the fuses, and I assumed that someone, bizarrely on Christmas Eve, was ironing. I flipped the switch and the lights came back on, including the oven light. Life resumed its merry pace. Aunt Margaret talked for England, my father helpfully washed up anything and everything he could lay his hands on, and the two old ladies went on shuffling by.

After about twenty minutes, I suddenly realised I couldn't smell the ham cooking. I opened the oven door. Stone cold. The element had blown. Twelve people were expecting three days of delicious food. I felt faint and sweaty. My father looked at me in alarm.

"I say," he said. "You've gone an awfully funny colour. Are you okay?"

The old ladies paused mid-shuffle, and even Aunt Margaret was silenced for thirty seconds. My life flashed before my eyes.

Just as Daddy was plying me with sweet tea and brandy, John came home laden with parcels, being one of the school who think Christmas shopping is best done just before closing time on Christmas Eve. He gazed at the tableau that met him. I explained what had happened. He thought for a moment.

"Is anyone in the street away this Christmas?"

"Yes, Frank Over-the-Road has gone back to Holland."

"Let's get his keys!"

We went to Maggie- Next-Door who ruled the neighbourhood with a rod of iron, and was a sort of street "châtelaine." We collected Frank's keys.

The next morning, it was pouring with rain. John and I set out in our dressing gowns and wellies, him bearing the turkey and me sheltering it with a large umbrella. Later, Aunt Margaret was stationed in Frank's kitchen to keep an eye on the roast potatoes and to give our ears a rest. When it was time for lunch, Aunt Margaret and I emerged from Frank's house. She clutched a large tray of roast potatoes and my knees buckled under the weight of an emu masquerading as a turkey. By this time, John had had far too many gin and tonics to be trusted with the turkey. Two men wending their way home from the pub gazed at us in wonderment as we scuttled from one house to another bearing the Christmas dinner.

So, all's well that ends well, except that poor Frank came home a day early, before we had had a chance to clean his usually pristine oven, and for a time he was quite concerned about the presence of a phantom turkey cook.

CHAPTER 13

During one reading with my darling Stephen, he told me there was a lady with me. She had beautiful blonde hair and, although I had no connection with her, she had come to help me. He said I would be meeting and entertaining very important and well-known people, and she would be my guide.

When I first met John, he had just moved out of a vast Edwardian pile in Hertfordshire. He said in no uncertain terms that he hated Edwardian architecture and that he had had enough of big houses.

"No you haven't," I said. "I can see a big house with a green front door. It has gravel in front of it, but it's a bit odd because the door is to the left of the house rather than in the centre."

After having been together for a couple of months, we went house hunting. We wanted to stay in Wimbledon as we both had friends there. I rang the local real estate agent.

"I've got the perfect house for you," he said, and named the road it was in.

"No, I really don't want to live there," I replied. "The road is much too busy and besides, the houses are much too small for our purposes."

"Not this one. Please, humour me. Just come and see it."

Because he was a nice, friendly estate agent, and because I had known him for donkey's years, I agreed to go and look at it. I arranged to meet him there. Imagine my astonishment when No. 17 turned out to be an enormous house with a gravel drive! It was, however, half of a huge pair of semis, and the green front door was to the left of the house.

We went into a grand entrance hall. To our right was the sort of staircase you should glide down in a ball gown, and on the half landing, catching the full afternoon sun, was a stained glass window depicting the signs of the Zodiac. How appropriate for me!

I fell in love with the house immediately, but I was convinced it was Edwardian and that John would hate it. We continued our tour.

"Do you like it?" asked the realtor.

"Um," I squeaked, too scared to say that I thought it was the most wonderful house in the world.

We went into the garden. I looked back at the house. There in the window of the master bedroom was a woman. She was wearing a Scarlett O'Hara type off-the-shoulder evening gown in the most beautiful shade of rose pink silk, and her thick, glossy blonde hair was dressed in intricate coils at the nape of her neck. She smiled at me.

Now, I may know zilch about architecture, but I'm a little more clued up about clothes. "When was the house built?" I asked.

"It's either late Georgian or very early Victorian," replied the agent.

"Thank God. In that case, we'll buy it."

The lady in pink was very partial to the half landing under the stained glass window, and I would often pass her on the stairs. She had a charming smile and never exhibited signs of anything other than a sweet nature.

I had met John at a lunch given by my friend Patti. She ran a very successful antique jewellery business and, because she worked six days a week, she employed a succession of au pairs to look after her children. Her daughter, Miranda, was at that time, best friends with Lulu. The girls spent a lot of time together and Miranda was like a second daughter to me.

I think if I had introduced a couple of friends who fell in love and set up home together, I would have been the first one on the door step with balloons and champagne, but poor Patti was going through a very nasty divorce with no Prince Charming in sight. I think this rather coloured her behaviour and, consequently, that of Miranda.

Patti had a very strange reaction when we moved in, for a long time refusing to cross the threshold. Everyone who came into that house was struck by its size and elegance, but when we eventually managed to drag Patti in kicking and screaming to give her the guided tour, all she would say was that the ceilings were high.

At the same time, Miranda started to get a bit iffy with Lulu. This was obviously very upsetting for Lulu, but I tried to explain that it must be difficult for Miranda. Our fortunes had undergone a marked improvement, whereas Miranda's life was in a state of upheaval with her parents divorcing and having to leave the home she had grown up in. Nevertheless, secretly, I thought they were both being a bit churlish.

One day Miranda came round and, as she and Lulu were going up to Lulu's room, I heard her say, "I don't know what all the fuss is about. I think it's a horrid house and so does my mum."

Fair enough. Not all tastes are similar, thank God.

About an hour later, I was preparing dinner when I heard an almighty clatter. I did the hundred yard dash from the kitchen to find Miranda in a heap at the bottom of the stairs.

"Darling, are you alright?" I enquired anxiously, heart in mouth. "Yes, I'm okay thanks, Sue."

"What happened?"

"The lady pushed me down the stairs."

"What lady?" I asked, knowing full well who she meant.

"The blonde lady in the pink dress on the landing. It's because I said horrid things about the house."

Well, well, well. Somebody else had seen her. I don't know what private thoughts Patti and Miranda still harboured, but I know they were never again openly insulting about the lady's home.

The house had a very peaceful, friendly air about it and I never once remember being the least bit scared. It was there, for the first time in my life, that I overcame my fear of the dark. Previously, I had always had to have at least a glimmer of light, but there I was happy to be in the pitch black. I knew the lady was watching over me and I felt very safe.

It wasn't quite the same for poor old Lulu on one occasion. John and I had gone skiing and left Lulu to guard the home front. Lodger John had gone home to Devon, leaving Lulu to her own devices. On the Saturday evening, she and a group of friends went to see *The Silence of the Lambs*. As they came out of the cinema, her friend Andrew turned to her and said, "I say, Lulu, didn't that cellar look just like the one at your house?"

Argh! Poor Lulu had to spend a solitary night thinking of Hannibal Lector in the basement. When she got home, she grabbed the aged retriever, put his lead on, and took him round the whole house, peering into cupboards and under beds. By the time they reached her room she had calmed down a bit, but the poor old dog was knackered. She locked them both in her bedroom, not emerging until it was light the next morning.

I think Lodger John was rather surprised by the warmth of the welcome he received when he got back that evening.

CHAPTER 14

I loved that house with a passion. I felt it was a part of me. I was happy, peaceful, and content, and felt as if I had truly come home. I would stroke its walls and talk to it as if it were a living entity. Even the Hannibal Lector cellar was a joy to me. Making up the old below stairs area there was a vaulted wine cellar, which was a joy to John as he could get his very expensive port back from the clutches of his ex-wife and her new partner who were happily roistering their way through thousands of pounds worth of tawny. There was a coal cellar and a pantry, but best of all was the old kitchen area, presided over by a strong-armed, red-faced cook who ruled over both her domain and minions with a rod of iron.

When I first got married in 1968, thanks to my mother's Belgian best friend, I could make an omelette and proper mayonnaise, but that was the extent of my culinary skills. I had no idea how to scramble an egg, so I bought two cookery books. One was by the doyenne of British food, Marguerite Patten, and I think it was a reprint of a post-war cookery book as it gave information on how to use powdered eggs and also how to get the best out of that newfangled gadget, a refrigerator! Anyway, it did the trick as it actually gave instructions on how to boil as well as scramble an egg.

At the same time, I bought another book which totally changed my whole outlook on eating - the wonderful Elizabeth David's *French Provincial Cooking*, which was a bible for any serious food lover in the sixties. This was at a time when olive oil was bought from the pharmacy in small medicinal bottles to soften ear wax, and garlic was mainly used for keeping vampires at bay. Madame David's vivid pictures of French kitchens and markets inspired me, and her description of a Provençale paradise as being far south enough for the olive tree to flourish but not far enough north for the Brussell sprout to grow, was one that will stay with me forever. Over the years, I had taken a great interest in cooking and was never happier than in the kitchen. When I am upset or just in a plain bad mood, I find the measuring and stirring involved in baking soothing and relaxing, so much so that the family get quite excited when I stomp off and lock myself up with my pots and pans as they know they will eat well.

Once I moved into that house, my cooking skills improved in leaps and bounds. John was a great foodie and we entertained lavishly. I thought nothing of catering four course dinner parties for twelve, or buffets for a hundred, preparing the type of food that would have scared the bejesus out of me at one time. I acquired a huge amount of confidence in the kitchen, knowing that a nineteenth century culinary magician was at my elbow.

At the same time, my psychic abilities were also becoming much stronger. Gradually the French coaching faded away to be replaced by an ever increasing number of readings. I think the house definitely helped me open up to the spirit world in a big way, and talking to Gran & co. definitely became much easier and more natural than in the past.

When I met John, he was not working. He had been the financial director of a large company that had caused, what was at that time pre-GFC, the biggest crash on the London Stock Exchange, and so he was "resting". When we first lived together, he told me a couple of people were coming to see him. I opened the door to two men who looked like FBI agents direct from Central Casting. I twittered around, pouring coffee and offering dainty biscuits, and then left them to it. It was only after they had gone that John told me it was the Serious Fraud Squad and that he was being investigated not only for his part in this débâcle, but also for a subsequent involvement with another company that had gone under in rather dodgy circumstances. He assured me of his innocence and they could never pin anything onto him, but, as you can imagine, he probably wasn't the most employable person around.

Luckily, he had had a generous golden handshake and lived high on the hog for a couple of years, but then he thought he had better look for a job. At that time, there was some sort of pyramid selling deal going on involving water filters. No dinner party was complete without one of the guests extolling the benefits of plumbed-in purified water.

A friend of a friend of a friend of John's was some sort of whipper-in for water filter recruits and we went along to one of their rallies. Terry was a gorgeous man. He was tall, handsome, and very charming, with stunning brown eyes you could drown in. He gave us such an inspiring pep talk that we all became quite evangelical and couldn't wait to spread the gospel to the non-filtered world. After the talk, John introduced me to him. My reaction surprised us all.

"YOU need a reading," I uttered, with uncharacteristic force. I realised what I had just said. "I'm awfully sorry," I stammered. "I really don't know why I said that."

John was turning puce.

"It's quite okay," said Terry. "I think you are probably right."

We arranged for him to come and have lunch with us in order to discuss water filters with John, and other matters with Gran. I set out the spread. My heart sank. I always try to be diplomatic, especially at the start of a reading.

"Are you having a few arguments with someone?" I asked. Terry burst into tears. I was on the right track.

He had two very distinct paths he could take. One led to money, happiness, love and all things good, the other to black despair. He had to make a decision; a decision that was simple to make, but difficult to put into operation. He knew what he had to do, but was fully aware of how hard it would be.

A few months went by. John and I and the lovely lodger, John Lavers, who was still with us, went to a football match at Wembley. After the match, we went for a curry – as you do – and out of the blue, I said to John, "Have you heard anything of Terry recently?" He hadn't.

About a week later, he came into the kitchen looking shocked.

"I can't believe it," he said, almost in tears. "Terry committed suicide a week ago. I think it was the day we went to the match. His daughter came home from shopping and found him hanging from the banisters."

"No!" I cried. "Poor, poor Isabelle!" This was Terry's daughter who was as bright, beautiful, and charming as her father, and already successful at a very tender age. She adored her daddy and I couldn't begin to imagine how she must have felt.

Over the course of that weekend, someone was desperately trying to get through to me. I was constantly being touched, my hair was being ruffled, and I was freezing cold. For a couple of days I couldn't work out who this extremely persistent spirit could be. Eventually, on Sunday afternoon, it dawned on me. I said to John, "I'm going to write to Isabelle."

"But you only met her for five minutes. She won't even know who you are." "It doesn't matter. I've got to write."

In the letter I said the usual things; how sorry I was and what a lovely man her father had been, but I finished by telling her how much he loved her and how proud of her he was. I sealed the envelope and went to the post box. The moment I mailed the letter, the touching and shivering stopped. Evidently, Terry had been trying very hard to get a message through to his much loved little girl and hopefully could now rest in peace.

CHAPTER 15

By 1995, I think it was only the house keeping John and me together. He was one of those men for whom the thrill of the chase was paramount, and after five years of living with his captured prey, the excitement had definitely begun to wear thin.

Around that time, I was introduced to a lovely lady who was in her late sixties and looked very much like Anne Bancroft. She had been widowed a couple of years previously and lived in a fine house with two Hungarian Vizslas and a Filipino housekeeper for company. She had just discovered the internet and had a high old time chatting up young men and, incidentally, knocking a good ten years off her age. She said to me one day, "I've gone from being good Jewish mother to cyber tart. I don't want a permanent relationship, I just want someone to send me yellow roses and give me a good seeing to!"

Whenever I went to visit, we would curl up in front of the fire, drinking Lapsang Souchong and I would swap her readings – tarot for tea leaves. At one such session, she said, peering into the dregs of my cup, "In February or March your knight in shining armour will appear."

"Is that John with a change of heart," I asked, desperate to rekindle a cooling relationship.

"I don't know. But do you know what? You won't even care," she replied. And I didn't.

At the beginning of January 1996, my friend Belinda and I were in my kitchen drinking coffee. I was bemoaning the latest shenanigans of John who had started shagging the local lady of easy virtue and telling me the most transparent lies to try and cover his backside. Suddenly, Belinda piped up, "You are going to marry someone called David."

"But I don't know anyone called David, and besides, I'm living with John."

"Sorry, it's definitely a David."

Now when I said I didn't know anyone called David, it was not absolutely true. Quite a few months earlier, John and I had been invited to a dinner party with another couple, David and Julie, who we had never met before. I was bowled over by David's silver hair and startling blue eyes, and we got on like a house on fire. However, I was with John, and David was with his soon-to-be ex-wife. I didn't have any further contact with him for about six months until just before Christmas 1995 when he called me to book a reading. His, by now, ex-wife had said he should consult a clairvoyant and had suggested "that woman we met at that dinner party." Surprisingly, John didn't take the news too well.

"What's he sniffing around for?" he asked. "I bet he doesn't want a reading at all. Well, I'm staying home this afternoon."

I told him not to be ridiculous, but maybe he sensed something.

When David came round, I started the reading.

"Do you have any business interests in France?"

"No."

"Do you have any connection with France?"

"No."

"Well, you will be working in France. You will be developing a property there. I can see a castle."

I went on with the reading.

"In February or March you will be courting a woman. She will be saying, 'No, no, no' but what she really means is, 'Yes, yes, yes.'"

David's eyes lit up. He was thinking about an old girlfriend who had been very important to him and with whom he had renewed contact after his divorce.

But Gran had other ideas.

As I looked at the cards, something very strange happened. I saw myself! This was unheard of. I never see myself in other people's readings. I did a reading for Belinda and I warned her that a very close friend was going to have a problem with his/her back. If he/she took care it would be alright, but if he/she took no notice of warning twinges, it could become very serious. Three weeks later she rang me as I was lying in my hospital bed, having been stretchered off in agony, unable to move anything south of my armpits.

"You daft cow," she said sympathetically. "It was you in the reading."

So, you can imagine my astonishment when I saw myself in David's reading. Feeling disconcerted, I decided discretion was the better part of valour and went to the loo. I managed to recover my composure and finished the reading, during which I told him quite a few other rather unlikely things which have, in fact, happened.

We met again at a party at the end of January. Unfortunately, the waiter took a bit of a shine to me and made it his mission for the evening to keep my glass topped up. Add to this the fact that I had undergone a personality change due to my hairdresser having a sudden rush of blood to the head causing her to dye my hair a rather startling shade of red, and you have the recipe for an interesting evening. I never used to tell anyone my political views, but, fortified by Chardonnay and hair dye, I was in full spate, railing against the European Union. David's ears started flapping like a bat's.

"I'm going to hear John Redwood speak at a meeting of the Bruges Group next week. Would you like to come?"

John Redwood is a Conservative MP who bears a strong resemblance to Spock in *Star Trek* and who, at that time, professed very strong leanings towards independence from the EU. I turned to John.

"David has asked me to go to a political meeting with him. Is that alright?"

"Of course. You love politics. You go," he replied.

Little did I know he was dying to offload me, in spite of his reaction to David's reading.

Off we went to the Westbury Hotel for the meeting, and then on to dinner. We talked for hours, but behaved in a very circumspect fashion. I did later tell John Redwood that he was our cupid, which caused him to look even more Spock-like than usual.

The following morning, I made my daily call to Belinda.

"I went to a political meeting with David Samuel last night." "David! David! I told you so! You're going to marry him!"

"Don't be ridiculous. I've only just met him."

"Don't care. You're going to marry him!"

My courtship with David continued a little like *Four Weddings and a Funeral*. We met at dinners, at barbeques, and at weddings, all the time becoming more and more attracted to each other, but all the time holding back as I was still officially with John.

A month before my fiftieth birthday, I decided to give myself a big party and, naturally, I invited David. At this point John and I were splitting up and my dearly beloved house was on the market.

By the time the party came, I was a work of art; massaged, plucked, dyed, and personal trained to within an inch of my life. All my effort paid off. The party was at the end of October, we had our first date on Armistice Day, 11th November, when I surrendered pretty damn quick, we got engaged on 21st December, and married the following April.

We had a rather unconventional start to our life together. When we became engaged, I was still living with John, and my solicitor strongly advised me not to move out of what was my house until the sale was completed. I was therefore in the strange position of living with one man whilst engaged to another.

As we got engaged so near to Christmas, I felt I should wait to announce it. As usual, we had a houseful of people for the festivities and

I really didn't want to put a blight on things. Somehow, God knows how, I had managed to get David invited. All the Christmas revellers knew about us except my father, John, and aged Aunt Margaret.

By this time, Aunt Margaret was nearing her telegram from the Queen, although this didn't stop her touching up my handsome young German teacher at Christmas lunch. She still had all her wits about her and kept casting baleful glances at David.

"Is he the waiter?" she asked repeatedly. Eventually, David couldn't resist.

"I'm definitely waiting," came the riposte.

By the time it got to Boxing Day, I couldn't keep the secret from my father any longer. "Daddy, I've got some news. I'm getting married."

"Darling, that's wonderful. Where's John? I must congratulate him."

"Oh no. Not to John. To David."

Just then, Belinda came into the kitchen.

"Has she gone completely mad at last?" asked my father in shock.

"No," replied Belinda. "It's the first sensible thing she's done in her life." Daddy thought for a moment.

"Good God! I don't have to pay for another wedding, do I?"

The following day, John and I left for a skiing holiday. He adored skiing and so I told David I would break the news to him on the plane on the way home as I was loathe to ruin his holiday – as I thought.

For months I had known he was having an affair, but he constantly denied it. The subject came up again on New Year's Day.

"I wish you would just tell me the truth," I said to him. "I know you have someone else."

"Well, I don't," he replied, tartly. "Do you?"

Perfect moment.

"As a matter of fact, I do. I'm going to marry David."

Now, I didn't exactly want blood on the snow, but a slightly miffed reaction would have been nice. Instead, I got, "Thank God for that. I didn't know how I was going to be able to get rid of you."

Problem solved. We went back home after the holiday and David and I came out of the closet.

We found a buyer for the house, and just before completion, John decided to take himself off skiing again, leaving me to pack everything up. I was pleased for two reasons. Firstly, because, helped by the lovely Don, I had free rein to organise a very complicated move with me, John, and Lulu going our separate ways, as well as stuff going into storage until David and I found a house. Secondly, and much more importantly, it meant that David could come and stay with me.

My gorgeous early Victorian house had very tall ceilings and was built on three floors. Lulu has a real penchant for hiding herself away at the top of houses and had colonised the top floor for her own little flat. One day, just before we moved, I went down to the kitchen to make an early morning cuppa. The part of the kitchen where all the main culinary activity took place was quite a narrow u-shape with an Aga cooking range on one side and all the tea making paraphernalia at the far end of this horseshoe.

As I waited for the kettle to boil, I thought about how lucky I was to have met David. Nevertheless, I had always had slight reservations about actually taking the plunge again. Every time I had come close to getting married in the past, something had happened unexpectedly to pull the rug out from under me. I used to blame husband John for this and would rail at him, shouting, "Why do you keep doing this? Why don't you want me to get married again?"

I made the tea, and with a mug in each hand, I turned to go back upstairs. Suddenly, there was a loud clonk and something metal bounced on the flagstones in front of me, as if it had been hurled straight down at my feet. I put the mugs on the work top and bent down. There on the floor was a wedding ring.

Now, I always wear Gran's wedding ring on the middle finger of my right hand. I checked. Still there, though how I thought it could have fallen off when I had been clutching mugs of tea, I don't quite know.

I picked up the ring and looked at it. It seemed familiar. Abandoning all thoughts of tea, I scaled the heights to visit the old bat in the attic.

"Do you recognise this ring?" I asked.

"It looks like Daddy's ring," replied Lulu. She wore her father's wedding ring, also on the middle finger of her right hand. "But, Mummy, I never take ... it ... off ..."

Her voice trailed away as we both looked at her naked hand. Somehow, John's ring had come off Lulu's finger, travelled down five flights of stairs, along a corridor, into the kitchen and ended up at my feet.

To be honest, we were both slightly freaked out by this. I didn't know what to make of it. I rang my other best friend, Sarah, and told her what had happened.

"Don't be daft," she said when I had recounted the story. "It's John giving you the wedding ring back. He's saying that he's giving you his blessing to marry David."

All those years I had been misjudging my poor dead spouse. He hadn't been trying to stop me remarrying, he had been trying to prevent me marrying the wrong person.

CHAPTER 16

Under any other circumstances, I would have been heartbroken to leave that house, but it was with a burstingly happy heart that I went to set up home with my beloved David. The sale of the house completed in March 1997, and for two months we lived in an adorable little house that he owned in North London until we moved into our own home.

There is a huge divide in London between north and south of the river. They are very different areas and the inhabitants of the one view the populace of the other with deep mistrust and suspicion. When I told my father I was going to live in North London, he panicked.

"My God! Will you be alright north of the river? Do be careful." He didn't exactly say, "There be dragons," but almost.

I was a little wary, never having ventured further north than Marble Arch, but I wouldn't have missed my time there for anything. One Sunday, without a backwards glance, I left Wimbledon after living there for thirty years. We set out in a three car convoy; David leading the way with a car full of stuff, me second with our large Golden Retriever, and Lulu bringing up the rear with the ironing board. She and I had no idea where we were going, so we screeched through a couple of red lights trying to keep up with David, who always drives as though his backside is alight!

We had a perfect start to our married life in our dear little doll's house. Obviously, David knew about my psychic work, but at first, in spite of his own reading, he was highly sceptical, although he respected my beliefs.

We hardly had any furniture as most of it was in store. We just had a table and dining chairs downstairs, so we tended to watch television in bed. As we had no curtains for the main bedroom at the front of the house, we slept in the small second bedroom with our large dog taking up most of the floor space and, traumatised by the change of scene, throwing up with alarming regularity.

David introduced me to the joys of *The Terminator,* and one night as we were watching Arnie save the world, David shot bolt upright.

"My God, I've just seen a ghost!" "What are you talking about?"

"I don't know. I just saw a figure sort of made of smoke go past the door." "Don't worry," I replied, still glued to Arnie. "It's only your grandfather."

I proceeded to describe the spectre in more detail. David was amazed, not only by the fact that he had seen something, but also because I had described his grandfather to a T.

These two months were one of the busiest times of our lives. Not only were we buying a house an hour south of London, but David was starting a new development in the north, so we spent a considerable amount of time driving between the two. We were also planning a wedding.

Not long before I left Wimbledon, I picked up the telephone one day to hear a flat northern accent saying, "My name is Mavis Parkinson. Can I come for a reading?"

"Of course," I replied, and booked her in.

From the sound of her voice and her name, I imagined an elderly Thora Hird figure in a grey cardigan. On the appointed day, about three quarters of an hour before Mrs. Parkinson was due, I was watering the garden, helped enthusiastically by the dog. Lulu came out of the house looking slightly shell shocked.

"Mummy, your client is here. I've put her in the dining room and offered her a cup of tea."

"Why are you looking so odd?" I asked. "You'll see," came the enigmatic reply.

I went into the house, having corralled the wet dog and dried us both off, and went into the dining room expecting to see a little grey-haired old lady. The most glamorous creature rose from her chair – a bronzed, blonde goddess, dressed all in white with many gold accessories, and hair drawn back in a topknot which rose at least six inches from the top of her head. The vision came towards me and held out its hand. "Ullo, I'm Maavis Paarkinson," it said in a broad Yorkshire accent.

Mavis had perhaps the strongest belief in the spirit world of anyone I've ever met. She asked for guidance from them (i.e. from me) about every aspect of her life at least three or four times a day. The calls would start about 8.30 am.

"Ullo, it's me. I've got a meeting with the bank manager. Psychically, what should I wear?"

Now, I have to be totally honest here and confess to some very unprofessional behaviour. I really didn't think that Gran & co. needed to be dragged away from whatever important activity they were engaged in on the other side to sort out Mave's wardrobe, so my answer was always the same. "Wear your cream jacket."

"Is that what you're picking up? Not the pink one? Or maybe the green and gold?" "No, definitely the cream. You look lovely in that."

It must have worked because she had the bank manager absolutely drooling over her and she somehow managed to wheedle enough money out of him to see her through a bad time. She ran very upmarket beauty salons, but before she met me she had been rooked out of quite a lot of money by a bogus Arab "Princess" who had offered her untold riches in return for a substantial down payment. She consulted me on every aspect of her life, and I think Gran and I ran her business for a couple of years.

I used to swap readings for her and her staff for beauty treatments. She had a couple of charming Iranian girls working for her, and the combination of European and Middle Eastern therapies she offered were out of this world. About three times a week I would brave the perils of north London traffic to reach Mave's pampering oasis. Consequently, by the time I married David, I was a work of art, a masterpiece, a poem, massaged, plucked, tweezed, primped, and varnished to within an inch of my life. Unfortunately for him, I lost touch with Mavis not long after the wedding and reverted to my normal state. I do still hope he didn't think he'd got a pig in a poke!

Our wedding was a wonderful affair. My first trip up the aisle had been rather fraught, what with Mummy organising the whole bash and Uncle Bert's black eye. To be honest, I had always felt rather envious of other girls' weddings. However, everything comes to she who waits, and the second time round was sheer perfection.

We got married at Cliveden, scene of the Christine Keeler affair back in the sixties. It is a magnificent stately pile and a wonderful setting for a wedding. The only trouble was that most of the guests were more interested in finding the infamous swimming pool where most of the scandal took place than in watching us get married.

David had not yet met any of my family, a very wise move on my part, and the idea was that Lulu would greet the guests at his side and introduce them. Unfortunately, although I never had the slightest doubt about marrying David, I got the most terrible attack of nerves and refused to let Lulu out of my sight. Consequently, poor old David was left to fend for himself. Luckily, I had had the foresight to make a list of the guests, accompanied with brief but scurrilous descriptions. All the old aunties were immensely impressed with David's ability to greet them by name. Thank God they never saw the list!

I eventually let poor old Lulu go, and my father and I made our way to the room where the ceremony was to take place. By this time, I was shaking like a leaf and hardly able to breathe. Handsome young men in morning suits were rushing around giving me glasses of water and brandy. My father, looking extremely elegant in a pale grey suit, held out his arm.

"Here we go again, chick," he said, as he half carried me down the aisle.

The moment I reached David's side, he took both my hands in his. The trembling stopped and all my fears disappeared completely. I had come home. I don't remember much about the actual ceremony, I just remember the palpable love between us and the look in David's eyes as we made our vows.

The sun shone, the champagne flowed. There was a slight food crisis due to the fact that one guest was seen scooping most of the canapés into her capacious designer handbag, but it didn't matter. That night, stars the size of dinner plates shone out of a velvet sky on the happiest couple in the world, and the following day, David carried me over the threshold of our darling doll's house to start our married life together.

CHAPTER 17

After a month of playing jeunes mariés in north London, we packed up the dog and ironing board again and set off for the delightful town of Alresford in Hampshire. Nearby is the village of Cheriton, where a famous Civil War battle took place, and for a while, the balance of power in Alresford swung between Cavaliers and Roundheads. Each time one of the armies was routed, they set fire to the town! When the fire reached our street, it spread along the houses, razing some to the ground, but just taking the roof off others. The house we lived in had originally been two houses, one of which was destroyed. It was rebuilt in the early eighteenth century and so we lived in a house that was half Tudor (the old house) and half Queen Anne (the new house).

Now, I don't know, dear reader, if you are familiar with the Tom Hanks film *The Money Pit*? When I first saw it, I laughed until I cried. David just cried. It is about a young couple who see a house that looks perfect. They fall in love with it, they buy it, and the house literally starts to fall down round their ears. They have to spend a fortune doing it up. Well, the only difference between us and them is that they were young.

The day we moved, being an efficient wife of four weeks' standing, I did the things one is supposed to do on moving day. I found the kettle and tea bags, I made up the bed, and started to clean our bathroom. The water in the basin was stone cold. I turned on the bath tap. Out came dark brown sludge. I let it run. The sludge got worse. By this time, we had a layer of silt about an inch thick in the bottom of the tub. I went to another bathroom. Same thing. I went in search of David, who was almost buried under a pile of packing cases.

"I think we've got a bit of a problem with the hot water," I informed him.

"I'll go and light the boiler," said my hero.

Now, David is the sort of chap who, if you mention DIY or gardening to him, goes rather white and pinched round the nostrils. However, he manfully set off to wrestle with the beast in the cellar. An hour and a half later he emerged, covered in soot and cobwebs.

"Sorry, darling," he said. "No bath tonight."

We had been told that the boiler would provide hot water but not central heating. As it was summer, the latter didn't worry us too much, but hot water was another matter. The next day, David rang the son of the vendor and asked if there was a knack to lighting the boiler.

"For Christ's sake, don't touch it!" came the reply. "It's lethal!"

I could have been a widow after only being a bride for a month!

We rang Mr. Sly, the plumber. Together, the three of us descended to the depths. We stood staring at the boiler, which stared malevolently back.

Mr. Sly sucked his teeth. "The whole thing needs replacing."

"How long will it take?" we asked, anxiously.

"I can get you a new one in three days."

Now, this was quite good news, but we were getting grubbier by the minute. We went into a café a couple of doors up the road. The owner was very sweet but kept looking at us slightly strangely. I felt I had to apologise for our appearance, so we introduced ourselves and explained our predicament.

"Oh, you poor dears!" she exclaimed. "Would you like to use the shower upstairs?" At that point we knew we had made the right decision to move there.

Things in the house got a lot worse before they got better. Every time we started to put one thing right, another went wrong. The previous owner had been partial to a bit of DIY, especially where the electrics and plumbing were concerned, and this, combined with bits of ceiling regularly falling on our heads and part of the roof caving in, just made it seem more like *The Money Pit* every day.

The demarcation between the old and new houses isn't overtly noticeable on the ground floor, but becomes more obvious on the first floor where a door on the landing of the new house opens onto steps leading down into the old house. At the end of the corridor and down another couple of steps is a bedroom with a second door leading to the back stairs.

When we had first been to view the house, the previous owner told us that there was a secret room behind the wall of this bedroom. She said her predecessors had opened it up, found a bed and a golden guinea, and then resealed it. The day after we moved in, David and the woodworm man attacked the wall. They tore off the woodchip paper to reveal a wooden framework and a door that looked like something out of a Tom and Jerry cartoon. It was crisscrossed with large planks of wood secured by huge nails, and the whole thing had been cemented shut. Nothing was going to escape from there!

The woodworm man produced a crowbar and made short work of the fortifications. The door came off to reveal another much older door with a latch. Everyone stood back.

"There you are, darling. This is your territory," said my Sir Galahad, pushing me gently forward.

I gingerly lifted the latch. I opened the door and peered in, expecting at the very least a pile of bones or the remains of a Puritan knocking shop. What a disappointment! No bed, no golden guineas, and certainly no bones. Just a small dark space. It had obviously been an old ostler's room as it had a trap door giving onto the original coaching entrance.

There was nothing the least bit spooky about it, but maybe we had unleashed something, because that room had a strange effect on people. I had strongly felt the presence of a Cavalier – well, there was bound to be one, wasn't there? I thought he had been wounded in his left shoulder and that maybe he had been sheltered by a Royalist household. I told David, but no-one else.

At our wedding, David had been quite startled by various women coming up to him and saying, "She doesn't come alone, you know? She's got all of us as well."

One even said, "She's a good woman and will cook you nice dinners."

All my friends were delighted when David and I got married, and very relieved to see me settled and happy at last. When we first moved in, the house was regularly invaded by hordes of women making the trek from London to see me, often causing David to seek sanctuary in his study. Naturally, we had to have guided tours of the house, including the aforementioned room, where they all experienced a similar reaction.

I have a fantastic friend called Carmel – a big girl with a huge personality to match. She is a no-nonsense Aussie and, both being Sydneysiders, she and David get on famously. She came down for a weekend and we did the obligatory tour. We went up the back stairs and into "the room". Suddenly Carmel doubled over, yelled, clutched her left shoulder, and promptly burst into tears, something extremely alien to her nature.

"Jeez," she exclaimed, becoming more Australian by the minute. "What the bloody hell is going on here?"

I quickly got her out of the room. I calmed her down and explained that it was the influence of whatever had taken up residence there.

"Don't be so damn silly," she retorted. "I don't believe in any of that."

We had a nice dinner, washed down by a good Australian Shiraz, and went up to bed. After about half an hour, David picked up his bunch of keys and crept out onto the landing. He tiptoed up to Carmel's door and shook the keys violently.

"David, you bastard, is that you?" queried my feisty friend.

No response from David.

"That is you, David, isn't it?"

The voice was getting a little less certain. No reply.

"David, please say it's you," she quavered.

David crept back to bed, shaking with laughter. The next morning at breakfast, she said to him,

"What the hell were you playing at last night?"

"Whatever are you talking about?" he asked, looking completely angelic and innocent. "Rattling things outside my door."

"I didn't rattle anything. I went to sleep as soon as my head touched the pillow."

Carmel blanched.

"Anything wrong?" he enquired, solicitously.

"No, not a thing. I must have been dreaming."

However, she didn't sound entirely convinced. The awful thing is that we never let on it was David!

"The room" was refurbished and Lulu decided that, being denied an attic, she would colonise the one with the ghost. We moved her furniture in and it made a charming room with an en suite cloakroom. The Cavalier no longer made his presence felt, either because of the new paint or Lulu, I'm not quite sure.

The first year we were married, we gave a big party to celebrate David's sixtieth birthday. Among the guests were two of his oldest friends who I had not previously met, a lovely couple called Christine and Tony. We had invited them to stay the night. As the rest of the house was heaving with assorted family and friends, I thought they might be happier slightly distanced from the madding crowd, and so I put them in "the room". The party carried on into the wee small hours but Tony and Christine went up to bed about midnight, having also been to a wedding in London earlier that day. What Lulu hadn't told me was that her bed was broken! Fine if you kept to starboard but a disaster if you rolled to port.

Tony and Christine settled down to go to sleep – and the bed broke! Now you can imagine how wide awake you would be at this point.

The next morning at breakfast, having been reassured that the accident was due to a faulty bed and nothing to do with him, Tony turned to David.

"I say, who was the young boy? Was it one of the caterers' children?"

"Oh, oh!" thought David.

"What do you mean," he asked, innocently.

"Well, as we were sitting up in the wreckage, the door opened and a young boy came in. He walked towards the bed, looked at us, and walked back out through the door."

"What did he look like?"

"He had brown hair in a sort of pudding basin haircut and he was wearing what looked like moleskin trousers and a coarse linen shirt."

For some obscure reason, David asked, "What did he have on his feet?"

Tony paled. "Do you know, he didn't have any feet!"

The next time we had a party, we again invited them to stay. They accepted, but declined the invitation to stay the night, saying they would stay in a local hotel, citing as an excuse the fact that they would have their two dogs with them. I don't know if we actually believed them.

CHAPTER 18

The word clairvoyant provokes very different reactions in people. There are those who look at me with a slightly pitying expression and cast furtive glances around for the men in white coats, all the while looking for a rapid escape route. There are times when I get the same treatment I imagine a gynaecologist does – I'm taken into a huddle in a corner and told gory details of the most intimate problems by total strangers. Or, having rather reluctantly, because of the aforementioned huddle, admitted my profession, I am then told that my fellow conversationalist is amazingly more psychic than I, but wouldn't dream of doing it professionally!

I don't think there are huge amounts of money to be made working as a professional clairvoyant. My understanding is that you are allowed to earn enough to live on, but not to make a fortune. In fact, I'm slightly wary of mediums who charge large sums for a reading, and I have known a couple who got greedy and had their gift taken away. People often ask me about lottery numbers, but it doesn't actually work that way. If there is no money involved, I can often pick out the winner of a race, but the minute I place a bet, you can be sure mine will be the horse bringing up the rear.

However, the spirit world does sometimes make itself very useful. The first year we were married, David took me to France for a week for my birthday. He had arranged for us to stay for two nights in a Château on the banks of the Dordogne, because he wanted me to wake up and go to sleep in a castle on my birthday. (See why I married him?) The hotel was like something out of a fairytale, and I thought what a lovely husband I had.

The birthday itself dawned fine and, although it was the end of October, the sun was shining and it was really warm. I knew France pretty well, but I had never been down to the south west before, having spent time mostly in Provence or on the Riviera. As had been countless Brits before us, we were charmed by the area and spent a very happy day pootling around. During our explorations, we came across the most beautiful house. It was not very big, but totally charming with an incredible view over the Dordogne. There was a chain across the driveway with a small notice on it – A VENDRE. It was for sale. David and I leapt into the car and hot footed it to the nearest village. We found a little estate agent. Just as we were about to go in, I said to David, "I don't know why, but I'm not going to let on I speak French," something very unusual for me. We went in and explained that we were interested in the house. Luckily, Madame spoke English. She burrowed in a pile of yellowing files and re-emerged clutching one to her ample bosom.

"Oh, I had forgotten about this," she said, blowing the dust off it. "It's been on the market a long time."

She took us to view the property and the more we saw of "Le Colombier", the more we wanted it. Negotiations went ahead. It belonged to a little old lady who had gone slightly dotty. Her son and heir had joined a strange religious sect and had set about converting the house into some sort of commune. On the first floor was a bathroom with a row of toilets and washbasins leading to a door which opened onto – a twenty-foot drop! When we enquired about the son, the agent replied, "He's not a problem. They've sent him to the Jesuits to get sorted out!"

We were very happy with our proposed residence secondaire, and whiled away many a happy hour discussing how we were going to do it up. However, one day, out of the blue, came a phone call to say that it had been bought by a notaire from Paris. We were devastated. It seemed so strange that a house that had been on the market for ages should have been snapped up from under our noses. In retrospect, maybe I should have trusted my initial instincts about the realtor and been more on my guard.

Nevertheless, the idea of a place in France now firmly rooted, we decided to continue our search. We saw a motley collection of properties, including one where I had a very noisy encounter with a bat, but nothing caught our fancy - especially not the house with the bats! David was insistent on having a view and eventually the agent said she had indeed got a property with a view, but we wouldn't like it.

"Never mind," said my hero, undaunted. "Take us to see it."

We turned and twisted our way along winding roads and through hamlets, and finally turned into a rather overgrown driveway. We drove for about half a mile and suddenly, rounding a bend, there was a château. It was magnificent, but best of all, you could see for miles.

"Why hasn't this been snapped up?" we asked incredulously, because the price was very reasonable.

"Wait until you get inside," replied the agent, rather ominously. "No-one can afford it!"

The château had been used as a Colonie de Vacances - a sort of summer school for the children of employees of a big national company. It had been fitted out with dormitories and shower blocks and was in need of total renovation and major building work. David and I looked at each other.

"We'll take it!" we chorused.

The building was much too big to be used as a private home, but as David was a property developer and I was a translator and teacher, we decided to pool our talents and convert the château into luxurious apartments with swimming pool and tennis courts.

We had a choice of architects. One was a local man with splendid moustachios who was very knowledgeable about the area. The other was a dour Scot who had been based in Périgueux for fifteen years. When I first met Ian, the Scot, I didn't warm to him. I tried to get David to go with the moustachios, but as he rightly pointed out, he could talk to Ian directly rather than having to go through me all the time. Looking back, this turned out to be a mistake as Ian was not quite as competent as he led us to believe and we had to sort out numerous problems. However, as I got to know him better I found him much more simpatico and thought my first instincts had been mistaken.

As the building works went ahead, I started to become concerned. "There's a problem with the lift," I said to David.

"What do you mean? It's not even in yet," he replied.

"I can't put my finger on it, but I'm very worried. It's dangerous and I can see people being killed."

I think David thought I was being a little fanciful, and assured me that the architect had it all under control. However, if I get totally fixated on something, I'm usually right, and I couldn't get rid of this awful feeling of impending disaster. Eventually David spoke to the architect.

"This may sound a bit odd," he said, "but Suzi has got very strong feelings that there is something wrong with the lift. I've seen enough over the years to know that there is something in it."

"I quite understand," said Ian. "My Grannie had the sight."

A couple of weeks later, he came to see us in England.

"Good morning, Mrs. Psychic Suzi," he greeted me. "There IS a problem with the lift. The bedrock is too solid to excavate the shaft down to the basement."

I was slightly reassured, but then the feelings came back stronger than ever.

I continued my nagging, until one day David came into the kitchen looking quite pale. "I've just spoken to Ian," he said. "The original charpentier (a sort of structural carpenter) has left and the new chap says that all the weight bearing calculations for the lift were wrong. The beam we were going to fix; it too could not have withstood the load. God knows what would have happened if Ian had not got him to check the figures carefully."

We installed a huge steel beam to take the weight of the lift and the feelings went away. David and I both said a word of thanks to Gran & co. for warning us in advance of what could have been a terrible disaster.

Another time, I said to Ian, "Please make sure that anyone working on the annexe roof wears a hard hat. Someone's going to fall off it."

We were having a new roof put on what was luckily a single storey annexe, and our macho roofers were not too partial to wearing hard hats in the heat. A few days later, we drove up to be greeted by the flashing lights of an ambulance.

"What's happened?" we gasped.

"One of the guys fell off the roof, but he's not badly injured because I insisted they wear hats," replied Ian. "They're just going to check him over."

But there was something I hadn't foreseen. When we bought the place, we were very relieved to find it was on mains drainage, something quite rare in rural France. We had been proudly informed by the local mayor that the system could cope with a hundred flushes at a time. The mind boggles! Anyway, we had no need to bother with any form of septic tank. Work on the annexe carried on and the builders turned their attention from the roof to the floor, digging down through the concrete to install some vital bit.

Ian rang us. "Had a bit of a problem today."

"What's happened now?" asked David in a resigned manner.

"Well, it turns out the annexe isn't on mains drainage."

"How do you know?"

"The guys were drilling today and when they broke through the concrete, they uncovered a massive septic tank under the floor. It must be at least a hundred years old and looks like it's never been emptied."

Nice!

"Unfortunately," he went on, "as they were drilling, one of the men fell in it."

"Oh my God," exclaimed David. "Is he alright? Did you take him to hospital for antibiotic injections?"

I have to say here that after fifteen years in France profonde, Ian had gone native and adopted the extremely non-politically correct, laissez-faire attitude prevalent in this part of the country.

"No, we just washed him down with a couple of pressure hoses. He's okay."

"Did you get it all off him?" asked David, worriedly.

"Don't know. It was a black guy," was the horrendously unbelievable reply!

Yet another time, we were being totally held up with registering some plans and couldn't fathom why.

"Beware the man in the black hat," warned Gran enigmatically.

Now, in France, if you want to register plans, you have to have an expert géomètre - in other words, a qualified measurer. Ours was completely charming, but whenever I asked when the work would be done, he always replied, "Within fifteen days, Madame."

Fifteen days used to come and go sans results. When I questioned him, I would get the same reply - we would get the measurements within fifteen days. Whenever I asked Gran what was going on, she would give the same mysterious response, "Beware the man in the black hat."

David and I couldn't believe our eyes when Monsieur le Géomètre turned up for a site meeting sporting an enormous black beret to match his enormous black moustache! Needless to say, the problem lifted when we got a new géomètre.

Working in France is not easy, and dealing with the rampant bureaucracy of French public companies is a nightmare. However, we battled through and finally finished the project, keeping one apartment for ourselves, the others being sold to people who wanted a holiday home.

The château was very isolated, and whenever we were the only people there, I had a feeling of unease, due in no small part to the invasion by hornets from the untreated nest nearby. We had had fly screens fitted, but the local carpenter doubled as the undertaker and was, I think, more skilled in making coffins than in fitting screens. At the bottom of every window was a gap of about half an inch. Perfect for the hornets to crawl through and terrorise me in the night. Every evening before bed, I would stuff towels along all the cracks and pray.

One night, I woke up at about 3 am to hear a noise. *Snuffle, snuffle, thump!*

"Bloody great hornet!" I thought to myself. I listened intently.

Snuffle, snuffle, thump!

It was right outside our bedroom window which was on the ground floor. I woke David - no mean feat in itself.

"There's a noise!"

"What sort of a noise?" he slurred, half awake. *Snuffle, snuffle, thump!* There it was again.

"That sort of a noise."

David listened for a while. The noise continued. He turned to me.

"Now, darling, I don't want you to be frightened, but I'm going to roar."

With this he let out the loudest roar that would have put the Lion King to shame. Even forewarned, I nearly shot through the roof, and obviously, whatever was outside had the same reaction because the noise stopped.

The next morning, we discovered the source of the snuffle, snuffle, thump. We found wild boar tracks right under our bedroom window. I have to say that what with wild boars and hornets, staying at the château wasn't a very restful experience and I was not sorry to say adieu to our home in France.

CHAPTER 19

During our marriage, David has never failed to be supportive of my work and has actually changed from being a dyed in the wool sceptic to a firm believer. He says he has seen and heard so much over the years, both first hand and from other people, that he is convinced of the existence of the spirit world.

He is, however, rather bemused by my fear of "ghosties". I have a passion for anything to do with the supernatural or serial killers – in itself slightly worrying – and I can and do read the most gruesome books, but when it comes to watching, that is another kettle of fish entirely.

Picture the scene. We settle down to watch TV and check the movie channels.

"Oh goodie," I pipe up, spotting the blurb for *The Haunting* or some such film. We switch on. I'm usually alright for a few moments, but the instant the incidental music starts to get the least bit creepy, I bury my face in David's shoulder.

"What's happening? What's happening?" comes the muffled shriek. "Well, look at it."

"No, I can't. It sounds much too scary."

This continues more or less all through the film. By now David has become resigned to having to give a running commentary. The film ends.

"Wow! That was really good!" I say.

I like to re-watch scary films, so little by little, I can watch the whole film all the way through. Somehow it's never as frightening the second or third time around. It did take me quite a few goes to watch *What Lies Beneath* uninterrupted, but now I don't even flinch.

Nonetheless, there a couple of things which still scare the socks off me. I don't know if certain scenarios touch a nerve or have some sort of relevance, but I am terrified by the old black and white Deborah Kerr film, *The Innocents*. When Quint appears at the French windows, I am to be found quaking behind a cushion. Unfortunately, in one house, I had very similar windows and at night they always scared the bejezus out of me!

The other book/play/film - and I know them all - that reduces me to a gibbering wreck is *The Woman in Black*. When Lulu was sixteen, she left her little school in Wimbledon and went off to Bryanston to do her A-Levels. I missed her dreadfully, and so planned a lovely treat for the Christmas holidays: a super lunch in London followed by a matinee. We chose *The Woman in Black*. When we got to the theatre, my suddenly grown up bunny said to Geoffie, my expensive luxury of days gone by, "I think we should put Mummy in the middle. She'll probably get scared." That seemed fine by me.

It was an excellent production. Lulu and I were quite happy until the end of the first act. The actress playing the title role suddenly appeared from the back of the theatre and glided silently down the aisle. Lulu and I screeched in chorus and nearly suffocated poor old Geoffie as we both made a grab for him. I can more or less guarantee this was the first and only occasion in his life he had been grabbed by two women at the same time!

When we went out for the intermission, Lulu ordered a double gin and tonic which she downed in one. Feeling slightly foolish, we laughed off our earlier reaction by saying it was just so unexpected and made us jump.

Fortified by our gin, we went back for the second act and I can honestly say that I have never been so frightened in my life. By the end of it, Lulu and I were quaking and hanging on to each other and to Geoffie for dear life, but we both agreed it was a fantastic play. I have seen the play a second time, as well as the TV film, and have also read Susan Hill's incredible book. Although I know exactly what is going to happen, it never fails to put the wind up me.

The town where we lived in Hampshire has an amazing firework display every 5th November and we were lucky enough to be able to see this from our house, which had a rather dilapidated self-contained flat on the top floor. One Bonfire Night, David said, "Let's go up to the flat. We'll get a better view from there."

"You must be mad," I replied. "I'm not going up there when it's dark." "Why ever not?"

"Because I'm scared of the ghosties!"

"But you deal with the spirit world all the time. It's as natural to you as breathing. Why are you scared of ghosts in the flat?"

"Different sort of ghosties!" I replied.

CHAPTER 20

Now, I am a glutton for punishment. Every Christmas for the past forty years, I have manfully wrestled with a twenty-pound turkey. Sometimes I win, sometimes the turkey wins, and on other occasions we call it a draw. Bugger the articles on how to look beautiful on Christmas Day. I emerge from the kitchen red-faced and sweating, fringe curling in the heat, covered in turkey fat, and staggering under the weight of a small emu. However, not only do I subject myself to the rigours of Christmas Day, which I love, but I always insist on an elegant black tie dinner on Christmas Eve. It's my Christmas present to myself to have dinner with my darling David looking so handsome in his dinner jacket. When the candles are flickering and getting low, and the wine bottles even lower, there is nothing I like more than to sit round the fire and tell ghost stories.

However, it's not so amusing when you personally experience the stories.

Not long after David and I got married, we set off on a trip down through France and Italy. We went in late September, thinking that, as schools were back, there would not be so many tourists about. Not a bit of it. We had pre-booked hotels as far as Rome and thought there would be no problem finding accommodation after that. The plan was to spend a couple of nights on the Amalfi coast and then head back up to Florence.

We enlisted the help of the hotel concierge, who spent ages ringing round his colleagues, but there was not a room to be had. All the good hotels were choc-a-bloc. Eventually, he called a pal at the Santa Caterina, a very posh hotel in Amalfi. Again there was no room at the inn, but he suggested we try a hotel called the Convento Luna in the town. Not quite so posh, but very good. Our concierge rang. Bingo! Their best room was available. We booked in for two nights and then turned our attention to Florence. Same problem. We could book into a fabulous hotel on the banks of the Arno, but not for the first night we wanted. Our trusty concierge, who by now was our new best friend, suggested we stay one night in Perugia. He was friendly with a concierge there and called in a favour, with the result that we were given a suite for the price of a double room

We left Rome, having profusely thanked and tipped our new best friend in equal measure, and headed off for Amalfi.

The Hotel Convento Luna was amazing. It was built right on the cliffs with only a road between it and the sea. You entered via a lift hewn into the rock, which took you up three floors to reception, and you stepped out of the lift into another world - a beautiful cloistered courtyard filled with the scent of jasmine and lemon trees. A peaceful oasis after the bustle of Amalfi.

Our room was a duplex looking directly over the sea. There was a sitting room with double height French doors leading onto a Juliet balcony. Upstairs was the bedroom, with a glass wall so you could lie in bed and look at the Mediterranean. The bathroom had been beautifully done. The shower cubicle had been carved out of the bare rock which had been left exposed.

After a very good dinner we went to bed and, already tired from our journey, we were soon asleep. At about 2.30 am we woke up. We could see the silvery reflection of the full moon on the water, so we got up and went down onto the balcony. As we were standing there, drinking in the beauty of the scene, I said to David, "There's somebody behind us."

David didn't react because it is quite a common occurrence. What I had felt was the presence of a monk dressed in a rough brown robe with a hood. He had his hands tucked into his sleeves and he was wearing a very distinctive rope belt. I couldn't see his face, just a matt black oval.

Having gazed at the moon for a while, we went back to bed.

I will always remember the next day as one of those perfect days, completely unaware of what lay ahead. In the morning we swam and sunbathed, and in the afternoon we hired a small boat with an outboard motor and puttered around the coast. Opposite the hotel, right on the edge of the cliff, was an old Saracen tower which the owners had converted into a restaurant, and that night we had a romantic candlelight dinner in the tower.

Again, at about 2.30 am I awoke with a jolt. David, although still asleep, had me by the throat, with one hand under my chin, about to break my neck. I yelled and he woke up and let go. He had been having a dreadful nightmare in which he had been fighting for his life and he had thought I was the enemy.

We were both thoroughly shaken by this. It's not every night you wake up to find your beloved husband trying to kill you. He went to the bathroom. When he came back, he looked shocked and pale, but I assumed this was due to the trauma we had just been through. He went back to sleep, but I stayed awake. For some reason, I knew I had to keep vigil and protect him.

Over breakfast the next morning, he said, "I had the weirdest experience when I went for a pee."

"Oh really?"

"As I was washing my hands, I looked into the shower and a monk was standing there."

I hadn't said a word to David about a monk, but he described exactly what I had seen, except that David saw glowing red eyes! We tried to ask the receptionist about the history of the place, but she became very shifty and would only talk about the film stars who had stayed there in the fifties.

We set off for Perugia. Now, David is an excellent driver having done a bit of rallying in his younger days, and we had spent a lot of time driving around Europe, but that particular day we just managed to avoid four near fatal crashes. Things got so bad that we decided to leave the motorway and head for Perugia on the back roads.

Perugia is an exquisite hill town that looks just like a film set for Romeo and Juliet. We checked into the Hotel Brufani. We were escorted to our room by a bell hop who proudly told us we were staying in the Queen Mother's room. Our Queen Mum? Yes! She had opened the hotel and stayed there for a couple of nights. We were shown into a magnificent apartment and, sure enough, in the bathroom hanging over the loo, was a portrait of our dear Queen Mother. Being such an ardent royalist, it tickled me pink to think I was parking my bottom on something that had been graced by the royal derrière.

With yet another dinner and good local wine under our belts, we toddled off to bed. The room was big enough to hold a dance in and, opposite the bed between two windows festooned with drapes, was an escritoire.

I awoke in the night to go to the bathroom. As I got back into bed, I saw the monk standing to the right hand side of the writing desk. Thinking I was imagining things, I dived under the covers and went back to sleep. I didn't mention it to David.

When we got back home, we were regaling my father with travellers' tales and we told him about the monk.

"Darling," said David, "what I didn't tell you was that I saw him again. I woke up in the night in Perugia and he was standing near the window just to the right of the escritoire."

I went cold. We had evidently brought this malevolent being along with us.

A couple of days later I spoke to my friend Maggie, who had spent quite a few holidays in Amalfi.

"Tell me about it," she said. "Was it lovely? Where did you stay?"

"At the Convento Luna. Do you know it?"

"Um!" She nodded.

"Have you stayed there?"

"No. We went for a drink once."

"Well, wait 'til you hear what happened to us!" "You saw a monk."
I was amazed.

"What! How do you know?"

"Because I saw him too. I was looking for the Ladies and he suddenly appeared. He was wearing a rough brown robe with a hood and a rope belt. His hands were hidden in his sleeves and I couldn't make out his face, it was all black. I was terrified and scuttled back to George. There was something so evil about that monk."

She had described in detail what David and I had both seen.

I did see him once in our house in Hampshire, and I prayed with all my might for Jesus to send him to the light. I don't know why he latched on to us, but we are both convinced he was responsible for the near misses on the motorway. I have vaguely felt his presence a couple of times over the years. As soon as I do, I call for reinforcements from the spirit world. I don't think he's with us anymore, but you can be sure I never relax my guard completely.

CHAPTER 21

Just after David and I got married, my father came to live with us. Mummy had died the previous year.

Where do I begin to describe this charming, clever, talented, cantankerous, stubborn, generous, selfish man? However I do it, I know it is done with an abiding love that no amount of difficult behaviour could ever destroy.

He was a brilliantly clever man and could turn his mind to almost any subject. At eleven years old he won a scholarship to Sir Walter St. John's School in Battersea where, as his old school reports bear witness, he excelled in everything except RE. Strange, as Gran was such a God fearing church goer – or maybe not! In those days, Battersea was not as posh as it is now and, although the school was excellent, the boys in their fine uniforms had to run the gauntlet of market youths pelting them with old lettuces. He passed his Higher School Certificate with distinctions in every subject, but, as the family's financial situation did not rise to university education, he joined an insurance company.

When the Second World War broke out, he joined the army, The Royal Artillery Company, and fought in North Africa and Italy, landing at Salerno and fighting his way north until being wounded at Monte Cassino. He was full of stories about his army career, in fact, I think he was a British Sergeant Bilko, "liberating" German jeeps, Italian wine, and God knows what else.

But he never talked about Cassino.

When he was a very old man, we offered to take him back there for the 60th anniversary. He put up all sorts of objections: he wouldn't fly, the journey by car was too far, he didn't want to go by train, all of which we overcame. Eventually, one day as I was having coffee with him, his eyes filled with tears and he said, "I'm sorry chick. I appreciate so much what you and David are trying to do, but I can't go back. I can't relive the memories."

We read accounts and memoirs of this hellish battle, but only those who have witnessed the full horrors of war can begin to understand what it is like.

Most of his stories only emerged after Mummy died and he came to live with us. It had always amazed me that such an educated and cultured man had never gone beyond the rank of private. He claimed it was because he didn't want to outrank his chums, but the truth was slightly different.

He had, in fact, been promoted to sergeant, and a couple of days after achieving his new rank, was detailed to drive an officer up into the hills near Cassino to see what was going on. They arrived at what seemed to be a deserted village and stopped in the main square. Suddenly people started to spill out of houses, hailing Daddy and the Major as liberators. They were pointing up the road and shouting "Tedeschi! Tedeschi!" "Germans! Germans!"

"Stay here, Hayman," said the intrepid Major. "I'll just go and have a recce."

By this time the villagers had produced copious supplies of wine and grappa. Now, Daddy wasn't the bravest of men, and the thought of the Bosch just round the corner prompted him to partake enthusiastically of the libations offered to the liberators.

Eventually the Major returned. "Okay, Hayman. Back to base." Daddy leered drunkenly back.

"I think you'll have to drive yourself, shir," he slurred.

The next day, Daddy lost his stripes and was sent to repair communication lines under fire.

His time in Italy was not without its high points. Whilst convalescing he met a pretty young school teacher who, among other things, taught him to speak perfect Italian. Luckily for me the romance didn't survive separation and he came back to marry Mummy.

He had met my mother while stationed at a training camp in Yorkshire. Their love somehow managed to survive both cultural differences and the war time flings on both sides. They married on 1st December, 1945, but Daddy was still weak from his wounds and found eating a real challenge. The old ladies – and there were plenty of them at the wedding, my maternal grandmother being one of thirteen children – took one look at his skeletal frame.

"Aye, it'll be a funeral next," they muttered.

Mummy and Daddy went to Scarborough for their honeymoon, an act in itself courageous in December. They stayed in the sort of boarding house run by a tyrannical landlady where come hail, rain, sleet, or snow, you had to be out by 9.30 am and not return until 5 pm. It was a brave person indeed who ventured back to face the Gorgon's wrath before the appointed hour.

One day they went for a walk, or rather a battle against the elements. Due no doubt to the bracing sea air, my father suddenly declared, "Gosh, I'm so hungry!"

Mummy needed no prompting. She was off like a startled whippet to the nearest fishmongers where she bought a Dover Sole the size of a small whale. Clutching her prize to her exceedingly ample bosom, she shot back to the digs and, brushing aside Cerberus, raced into the kitchen, cooked the sole, and presented it to Daddy who gobbled it down. This was the turning point. His appetite came back with a vengeance, as did his strength. I was born the following October, and family lore has it that I am the result of that Dover Sole in Scarborough.

They lived in London with Gran and Grandpa, and Daddy went back to the insurance company. He always had a very strong interest in politics. He was an unswerving member of the Conservative Party until the day he died, in spite of his violent disagreement with their ever growing involvement in the European Union which he hated with a passion. After the war, he became a party activist, being Chairman of the local Tories and standing in local council elections, a rather thankless task in solidly Labour Balham. Whenever there was an election of any sort, our house served as the committee rooms. When I was a baby, many a young Turk was given the job of getting me to sleep, and I am told that one in particular, who later rose to political prominence, used to practise his speeches while rocking me to sleep. Maybe that explains my own passion for politics.

My father was a complex man, never wishing to push himself forward, but at the same time arrogant in a rather self-deprecating way. He was extremely musical and had a great love and knowledge of opera.

He played the piano, Rachmaninov being the favoured composer, and any lack of technical ability was more than made up for by his passionate interpretation. He sang beautifully and had been talent spotted in Rome and asked if he would join the Rome Opera Company. This would have been an incredible opportunity and I could never understand why he turned it down.

My mother was an ambitious, demanding, and difficult woman whose role had to be centre stage, and at home Daddy always took a back seat. All through the sixties she led him a merry dance. When I was eleven she decided to go out to work, something very unusual in those late fifties days of happy, smiling, repressed housewives, and she got a job as secretary to an Earl who headed up a steel company. It was through this job that she met a lot of powerful and rich men and, bamboozling my father and me with excuses that it was business, would sally forth in all her finery to have dinner with one or other of these magnates. She would return home at 2 or 3 am, much the worse for wear, and then complain the next day how tired all this overtime made her! On the surface, my father accepted all these tall tales, but who knows what was filed away in his memory bank.

The years started to take their toll. Mummy's glamour began to fade, and the boyfriends became more down-market. Unfortunately, her mind started to deteriorate with what we later found was the onset of Alzheimer's, helped along by all the gin that had been consumed over the years. As the Alzheimer's began to take hold, my father took on the role of carer, hiding from the outside world, me included, how bad the problem was becoming. His behaviour was irreproachable. He covered up a lot of her lapses, prompted her when she was talking, and seemed to be the perfect protective husband. The worse she got, the more caring he became until his treatment of her was positively angelic.

However, behind closed doors, the role of carer and a privately concealed resentment took their toll.

CHAPTER 22

When he came to live with us, he was in quite a sorry state. However, the newly liberated Ronald gradually perked up and joined a group of frightfully Okay ladies who used to meet for a pink gin every Friday lunchtime. My father was a very handsome, distinguished-looking man. In his youth he was often mistaken for the actor David Niven, and even in old age he was still a very attractive man of infinite charm. He certainly set the old ladies aflutter.

"Dear Ronald is so charming," they would say, fanning themselves.

To most people in the town he was known as "Daddy". I don't think he minded this too much, although he did occasionally mutter darkly into his moustache that he would have to start signing his cheques "Daddy".

Not long after his arrival, we were talking about holidays and he announced that his travelling days were over. David and I had to go to France quite often to oversee the building project, and Daddy used to say how much he would have loved to have seen the chateau, but feared he was now too old and doddery. Now, David doesn't know the meaning of the word "can't" and decided we would take Daddy down with us on our next trip. When the time came, we installed him in the back of the car, all comfortably tucked up with a couple of cushions, and set off.

We found that the best way for us to make the journey was to catch the early morning ferry from Southampton, get a cabin, read the papers, have a sleep for a few hours followed by an early lunch on the boat, and then drive from Le Havre to Martel - the way David drives it was a journey of about five hours. Daddy was fine. He loved being in France again and took great delight in using his excellent French to charm the patronne of the hotel where we stayed while building works were being carried out.

"Monsieur est très charmant," she would tell me, fanning herself.

He came down with us a few times and became a well-known figure in our little local town, but by 2003, the last trip he took with us, he had become rather frail and felt that to do the journey in one hit was a little taxing. He suggested we stop somewhere for the night and offered to pay for a nice hotel for the three of us.

"*Whoopee do!*" I thought, and beetled off to get my Relais et Chateaux book to sort out a bit of luxe for our stopover. I have to point out here that my book was a bit old, but nonetheless I scanned through it and found a hotel about halfway into our journey. It looked beautiful, and so I rang and booked for the following Monday.

We set off, my posh frock on a hanger in the back of the car in readiness for the expensive dinner in an elegant restaurant that I thought lay ahead of us. When we arrived at our destination, we had a bit of trouble finding the hotel. After a few circuits of the town we discovered it in an old cobbled street we had already driven down a couple of times before, opposite the huge chateau that dominated the town. There was a small sign over the entrance, which was set into an ivy-clad wall. We drove through a pair of massive old oak gates and down a gravel drive between the two wings of the hotel.

My heart started to sink. You could see the hotel had once been exquisite, but now it had a dilapidated air. The paint was peeling off and, although the roses were still valiantly blooming, the gardens were overgrown and the lovely ornamental pond was covered with green slime.

We drove down to a parking area and David stopped the car. Suddenly, a woman appeared beside his door. She greeted us and welcomed us to the hotel. We got our bags out of the car and I took my posh frock, feeling I had been slightly over optimistic.

Madame took us into one of the wings of the building. The entrance was impressive. An elegant marble-floored hall the size of a ballroom with alabaster statues in niches led to a wide staircase. She said our rooms were on the first floor, but when I asked, she told us there was no lift. I explained that my father could not manage the stairs.

"Pas de problème, Madame," she said. "I can give him a suite on the ground floor." She led us down a corridor and opened the door to what was the equivalent to a reasonable-sized flat in London. It was luxuriously furnished, but had a rather unused air about it, and a slightly musty smell.

Daddy was in his element in such splendour, as happy as a pig in clover. We left him to sort himself out and went up to our room. It wasn't quite as big, but nevertheless a very generous size with a separate sitting room. Again, there was the air of faded glory. The bathroom was like something out of the twenties. It reminded me a little of the original ladies' room at the Ritz in London, but the tiles and mirrors were definitely in need of a bit of refurbishment.

Daddy and David had arranged to meet for a beer while I glammed myself up, but having seen the entrance, I thought I would join them to suss out the place before putting on the good gear.

We went down into the courtyard. Madame brought our drinks and then said, "I'm sorry, the chef isn't here, but I can cook you something."

"Is that because it's Monday (when a lot of places close in France) or is he off permanently?" I enquired.

"Oh, because it's Monday," came the quick reply. "But I can offer you foie gras and then sturgeon."

Sturgeon? Wasn't that a royal fish? Were we about to commit the fishy equivalent of Swan Upping? I had never thought of sturgeon as being good for anything except caviar, and besides, it was hardly the sort of thing you'd have kicking around in the fridge in case someone popped in for supper.

"That would be fine," I said.

A young man dressed in jeans and a t-shirt came over, and the woman introduced him as her son who was the maître d'hôtel.

"I apologise for not wearing a dinner jacket," he said, "but it's Monday."

We assured him he was fine just as he was, and with great ceremony, he ushered us to dinner. I had given up all hope of the posh frock.

As with the rest of the hotel, the dining room had been lovely, but the paper was starting to peel and one of the shutters was hanging off. The table was beautifully laid with spotless starched white linen and gleaming silver, and light from candles danced in crystal glasses. The foie gras arrived, and Monsieur, sans dinner jacket, produced a couple of fantastic wines to accompany the meal.

I have to say here that my father was, by nature, quite abstemious. He liked a glass of good red wine, but never overindulged and was by no means a toper.

This particular evening, he drank like a fish, downing the first glass in one go. Somewhat bemused, the maître d' poured him a second.

"Fill it up," said Daddy, insisting it be filled right to the brim. David and I regarded him in astonishment as the second glass disappeared as rapidly as the first.

"Can't you see all the ladies and gentlemen in their old fashioned costumes walking up and down outside?" asked Daddy, a question that, at the time, we took to be rhetorical.

After the excellent foie gras, we had our sturgeon, which proved to be delicious, followed by cheese and pud, and due to the food and wine, we were feeling no pain.

"Would you like a digestif?" enquired the maître d'.

"An extremely large Armagnac," ordered my father.

"I would like a Grand Marnier, please," I said, somewhat timidly.

"Certainly, Madame. Which would you prefer?"

This was a new one on me as I had only ever seen the ordinary old Grand Marnier. "We have a forty-year-old, a ten-year-old, and a non-vintage."

Now, I didn't think in all honesty I could sting the old boy for the forty-year-old one, but felt his budget could well stretch to the ten-year-old. The waiter showed me the bottle. On the label was printed 1972, but I really didn't think too much about it at the time.

We finished our drinks and stood up to leave, Daddy waving slightly in the breeze. I tucked my arm firmly into his and started to frog march him back to his room. As we tottered down the gravel, we unexpectedly veered to the left. I clutched Daddy tighter as I tried to stop him disappearing into the roses. Suddenly and silently, Madame appeared at his side. She took the other arm.

"I will help you. Allons, Monsieur!"

We got Daddy into bed and David and I retired to our own spacious quarters.

The next morning, the three of us assembled in the courtyard for breakfast, Daddy looking surprisingly perky without a trace of a hangover. As we were happily chomping through a pile of croissants and homemade jam, an old fashioned laundry van drove in. Madame appeared, trundling one of those huge canvas linen containers on wheels like you see in hospitals. Now, apart from us, the place was deserted and it was obvious that nobody had stayed there for some time, but there must have been about thirty sets of used sheets and towels in the basket. The laundry was loaded onto the van which then drove off, and the gates were closed behind it.

We finished our breakfast and my father wanted to settle the bill. Madame seemed to have disappeared. I went into the reception to try and find her. On the counter was the most wonderful old fashioned till with huge keys and a pop out cash drawer. Still on the hunt for someone to take our money, I went through a door and found myself in the most enormous kitchen. I looked around. All the fixtures and fittings were very old fashioned and the fridge and cooker looked like something from the seventies. The place was pristine apart from a layer of dust, with no sign of any dinner or breakfast having been prepared.

I went back into the reception and there was Madame perched on a high stool behind the till.

"My father would like the bill, please," I said. "Certainly, Madame. Right away."

When the bill arrived, Daddy peered at it. "Good Lord," he said. "That's extremely reasonable. I can't believe we had all that for so little."

He paid the bill in cash and Madame rang it up on the till. When she brought him the receipt, she gave me a small folder. "A little present for you," she said.

I opened it up and inside was a hand-embroidered lawn handkerchief. I hadn't seen a handkerchief for years, let alone a hand-embroidered one.

"How very kind of you. Thank you," I said.

"Just so you won't forget us," replied Madame.

We made our farewells and crunched our way down the gravel drive. We loaded up the car, got Daddy tucked up in the back with his pillows, and put on our seat belts. Madame opened the gates for us and we drove out. We stopped almost immediately to look at the directions she had given us to get back to the motorway. I happened to glance back. The gates had been firmly shut again and the hotel seemed to have shrunk back behind the ivy clad wall. We set off feeling rather quiet. I thought David looked a bit odd.

"Are you okay?" I asked, thinking maybe the strange expression was something to do with last night's sturgeon.

"I think so," he replied. "But, do you know, I just realised the strangest thing. When we walked on the gravel we made a heck of a noise, but whenever Madame appeared, she was completely silent. And also, did you notice the date on that bottle of Grand Marnier? It was supposed to be ten years old, but it was marked 1972."

We looked at each other. Where had we been staying? What had happened at the Hotel Espagne? Had we stumbled into a time warp? Had my father actually seen "all the ladies and gentlemen in their old fashioned costumes walking up and down outside"? That would certainly have explained the amount of alcohol he quaffed.

When I got back home, I got myself an up to date Relais et Chateaux book, plus a new Michelin guide. Not a trace of the hotel in either, or indeed in any other guide book I could find.

I have often thought about going back to try and find out more about the hotel, but I have resisted the temptation. I like to think of it as a sort of Gallic Brigadoon, appearing out of the mists every so many years. If I discovered it was just an ordinary, run down place, it would be a great disappointment. On the other hand, say I went back and found that it had burnt down in 1982?

Welcome to the Hotel California!

CHAPTER 23

It seems a lot of psychics have Red Indian (sorry, Native American) guides. The number of people I have consulted or spoken with who are guided by Grey Owl or Running Bear is impressive, although I do remember watching a brilliant psychic

Scotsman on TV who said that if there are so many Indians out there, there must be an awful lot of cowboys! Well, I don't have Red Indians, I have grannies, and let me tell you, they could give Grey Owl a run for his money any day!

Gran is such an integral part of my life that I can't imagine her not being around. She is my main guide. She is the one who watches over me and helps me with readings. If I'm in trouble or need advice, it is always Gran I turn to and she usually turns up trumps.

Whenever I have consulted a clairvoyant, the first thing they say to me is, "Who is Emily?" There is, however, the exception that always proves the rule. On the advice of a couple of friends, I went to a certain spiritual association for a reading. This was like a psychic production line. The basement of a beautiful Georgian house had been converted into a rabbit warren of little plasterboard cubby holes into which clients were shunted for exactly thirty minutes, after which a kitchen timer rang and we were shunted out again.

My appointed medium was a rather unfortunate rotund little chap with an air of Uriah Heep humility about him. I sat through half an hour of what I can only describe as clap trap. I could relate to absolutely nothing. He kept telling me a man was with me, which might have been true, but I could see no relevance at all. Nonchalantly, I enquired if he could see a woman with me.

"Oh no, dear," came the reply. "No women around you."

I looked at Gran shaking like a jelly, tears of mirth rolling down her cheeks, our bonsai charlatan completely unaware of the actual spirit just behind him.

She is terrific about most things, but one thing she is not awfully good at is scoring goals. I am a great Manchester United fan and even have a No 7 Eric Cantona shirt which, you will be relieved to know, I only wear in the privacy of my own home. I love watching footie on television, but I tend to get a little carried away, jumping to my feet from time to time screeching, "Offside!" or "Referee!" and scattering husband, dog, cats, and various potted plants in my excitement. My poor husband had no idea he had married a football hooligan until after I'd got the ring on my finger. One evening I was watching my brave lads playing Chelsea and they were trailing sadly.

"Come on, Gran," I urged. "Get them to score a goal."

With that, one of the Chelsea forwards neatly booted the ball into the net.

"Wrong team, Gran. They're the ones in red, not blue."

"Sorry, dear. I'm afraid I don't know very much about football."

She is absolutely brilliant at finding parking spaces. It seems to be her forte. When I was first dating David we went to Covent Garden Opera. David, quite understandably for anyone without a handy gran, was very concerned about parking.

"Don't worry," I said. "Just drive as near to the Opera House as possible. We'll find a space."

Giving me one of those 'I guess I'll have to humour her because she is quite sweet and we are in the first flush' looks, he duly drove right up to the edge of the pedestrian precinct.

"Darling, I told you it was impossible," he said. "I'm afraid we'll have to park further away and walk."

Walk! Not if I could help it! Gran understood all too well the problem of having to hoof it in killer heels and, just as David was turning the car round, someone pulled out of pole position.

"Good heavens," said David. "That was so lucky."

"That wasn't lucky, that was Gran."

"Gran?"

We were in the very early stages, and although Gran strongly approved of this handsome Australian, they hadn't been formally introduced.

"Yes. My grandmother always finds me a parking space."

At the time he gave me a look which was equivalent to a pat on the head and a 'there, there, dear', however, over the years he has seen how she always manages to find a space. She's especially good around Peter Jones and Harrods as she has always been quite partial to a bit of shopping.

Sceptical Joyous, my boon companion of the Mrs. B saga, was extremely impressed with this ability.

"I wish I had someone to find me parking spaces."

"Well, borrow Gran. She'll help."

So now, every time Joy goes to Kingston, she says, "Please, Suzi's gran, find me a space," and Gran always obliges.

She was highly delighted when I met, fell in love with, and very swiftly became engaged to David, my handsome, charming Australian with a huge intellect and a great sense of humour. We married in 1997 and have been blissfully devoted to each other ever since.

I think Gran might have had a hand in this as our paths had very nearly crossed before. David's ex-wife, before she became his wife, lived just across the road from my parents and, in fact, David lived there for a few months whilst their new house was being renovated. It also came to light that his step-daughter had briefly been in my daughter's class at a tiny private school in Wimbledon. As I was "Den mother" and on all the school committees, David and I must have met at fundraisers or parents' days as I was usually the one going round trying to get rid of the guacamole and slightly tired crudités. At last, thanks to a dinner given by unexpected mutual friends, she succeeded in engineering our meeting, and thoroughly approved of her Antipodean grandson-in-law.

After several years of marriage, David persuaded me to overcome my fear of flying and go for a lovely holiday to Australia. I do travel by plane, but I'm the sort of passenger you would hate to have in the seat next to you. I pray a lot and I drink a lot, and God help my neighbour if it gets bumpy. I have been known to leave bruises on complete strangers.

Anyway, thanks to David's powers of persuasion and the added inducement of Qantas Business Class, off we set on our excellent adventure.

The stage management of my introduction to the city was worthy of an Oscar. We landed at around 6.30 pm and took a taxi to the Hyatt at The Rocks. This didn't mean an awful lot to me as I was totally ignorant of the geography of Sydney at that time. The taxi drew up to the main entrance and we checked in. It is a lovely hotel, but I had no idea what was in store for me. We followed the bellboy to our room, but as he opened the door, David took my hand.

"Close your eyes and promise not to look until I tell you," he said.

He guided me forward. My eyes were tightly shut. He stood behind me and put his arms round me.

"Open them now."

I could not believe the view spread out in front of me. There was the famous bridge! There was the Opera House! There were the ferries and the reflections of the lights of Circular Quay twinkling on the water! It was a magical introduction to a magical place.

We were mainly based in Sydney, David's home town, but we had decided to travel around and see as much of the country as we could during our six week stay. We intended to drive up the Pacific Highway as far as Cairns to visit The Great Barrier Reef.

Before we left we went to a dinner party hosted by our good friends Pats and Bill. I had first met Pats in Wimbledon when our girls were small, and she and I had become great pals. Bill was a dentist from Queensland and, after a stint with the Flying Doctor Service, had moved to England in the seventies where as part of his practice he had been the dentist to Chelsea Football Club. I was sorry when they moved back to Oz and was delighted to meet up with them again.

During the dinner party, we talked about our forthcoming trip.

"Oh my goodness!" exclaimed one of the guests. "You'll be able to see the Big Banana."

I was slightly startled. Was there some slightly louche connotation of which I was unaware?

The other guests got quite excited. "Yes, it's great!"

"That's really something to see!"

"I really loved the Big Banana!"

I dared not ask. David was looking decidedly uncomfortable, albeit smirking slightly, wondering if I had been overly forthcoming about intimate parts of our life.

I need not have worried. There is actually an exhibit of a giant banana in northern New South Wales. In other areas you can find the Big Prawn, the Big Merino, the Big Pineapple and, on one memorable occasion, the Big Cauliflower. Perhaps not as exciting as I originally imagined, but nonetheless, the Big Banana is a tourist attraction.

As we journeyed north, the country became more tropical. Queensland is a state of sugar and banana plantations fringed with white sand beaches and palm trees, its shores lapped gently by the turquoise waves normally only seen on travel posters. We stayed at Airlie Beach at the start of the Whitsunday Islands where I leaned over the balcony to see turtles swimming in the clear azure sea.

We drove to Port Douglas to visit the Great Barrier Reef, an unforgettable experience I would highly recommend. To tell the truth, although I am a very strong swimmer, I am a total coward when it comes to swimming in the sea, especially in Australia where I imagine hordes of great white sharks lurking beneath me. Luckily, the tour organisers cater for cowards like me. You can go down in a submersible and still see everything in comparative comfort without fear of jellyfish or Jaws!

We stayed at a super plush resort in Palm Cove for a few nights. We strolled hand in hand along the moonlit strand from the hotel to the jetty. There was a notice warning people not to walk their dogs along the beach as the salt water crocodiles came up on the sand at night and might snaffle the pooches for a midnight snack. That was the last time we walked along the beach!

During our stay in Queensland, we decided to explore the rainforest and find a couple of waterfalls that were meant to be spectacular that David particularly wanted to see. We left the coast, drove up hairpin bends through lush tropical vegetation, and finally emerged onto the tablelands of North Queensland. We found our way to the site of the first waterfall and parked the car. There was a large signboard, on which was prominently displayed a picture that looked suspiciously like Big Bird from Sesame Street along with the warning for us all to beware of cassowaries. It was their mating season and it looked as if they got a bit bad tempered if thwarted - rather like most men!

Having practically bathed in insect repellent, I set off intrepidly through the jungle with David, casting the odd glance into the bushes for frustrated cassowaries. As we walked along the trail I began to get uneasy and felt rather queasy.

"What's wrong?" asked David.

"I don't know, but I don't like this," I replied. David laughed. "Don't worry, I'll protect you from over-amorous birds."

I tried to explain that it had nothing to do with birds, but he kept cackling and making feeble jokes about birds with or without feathers.

As we were walking along the trail we met another couple coming the other way. We stopped to say, "G'day."

"Have you seen the bottomless pit?" they asked.

Never heard of it.

"It's well worth the extra walk."

We decided to see that before we went to the waterfall. As we drew near, the feeling of unease increased. We came out of the jungle shadows into the sunlight. There was a viewing platform built out over the void and we went on to it. There before us was a huge crater about two hundred feet deep. It had totally sheer sides and was filled with water covered with what looked remarkably like pond weed. As I looked at the top of the cliffs surrounding us, I became aware of bodies falling, being pushed into the water. I heard the screams as people plunged to their death. I walked off the viewing platform feeling sicker by the minute.

I had always thought aborigines were gentle souls who lived off the land and told tales of the dream time, but the picture I was getting was anything but gentle.

"Were there any warlike aborigines?" I asked David.

"Oh yes, especially up here in the north," he answered.

I suddenly realised that this was a place of sacrifice to dark gods.

We left the pit and walked toward the trail to the waterfall. By this time I was literally filled with dread.

"Please don't go to the waterfall," I said to David.

"Don't be daft. That's why we're here."

"Please, I'm begging you." I was beginning to get slightly hysterical.

"Okay. I'll go on my own if you're scared."

"No," I screamed, hanging on to his arm for dear life. "It's you. If you do go down that path you'll die!"

At this point, David did think something was up. Whether he believed what I said or whether it was the thought of carrying his fainting, hysterical, slightly portly wife back to the car, I don't know, but he did give in. However, as you can imagine, he wasn't too happy about not seeing the waterfall.

We drove on to the next one with him muttering darkly, "Bet it will be the same when we get there! Bet I won't see this one either! Just 'cos she's scared of birds!"

We got there and parked. Again, I showered in insect repellent. Again, I peered at the poster for frisky Big Bird. We set off, this time not on a wide, well-maintained trail, but on boardwalks built down through the forest. I loved it!

I revelled in the sights and sounds that half an hour earlier had seemed so threatening. The waterfall was magnificent and I eventually had to be dragged away. All feelings of terror and physical malaise had gone.

Now, I can't know if anything would have happened to David at that first waterfall. All I know was that I had the very strong feeling that if he went down that trail he would die. And believe me, there was no way I was going to take the chance that I was wrong.

CHAPTER 24

When David was seventeen, his parents came over to England and he spent a year with his grandparents, Prucel and Morrie, in Perth. Morrie had made his fortune in Kalgoorlie during and after the gold rush and had whisked his bride off to live in what was then a real frontier town. Prucel was made of stern stuff. She created a beautiful home, and David's father was born during their time there. Having made a decent pile of money, Morrie moved his family to the elegant suburb of Claremont on the Swan River.

During our visit to Perth, we went to Claremont to try and find the house where they lived, and where David spent time with them. Claremont is a lovely area with houses that look like something out of *Dallas*! When we found where the house was, it was no longer there, having been replaced by three very grand piles. Luckily, the house next door had been turned into a museum and we found photos of the original house and tennis court. The latter, much to David's disgust during his sojourn there, had been given over to duck rearing.

It was during this visit that the second grannie came into our lives. Prucel. She started off quite low key.

"Did Prucel have a special part of the garden where she liked to sit?" I asked.

"No, I don't think so. She preferred to sit on the verandah."

"But she keeps telling me about her garden. She must have loved it. Was she interested in gardening?"

"Not really. She had someone to do that for her."

Heigh ho! You can't win 'em all. I must have been imagining things.

We decided to explore a bit more of the Samuel family history during our West Coast visit, and so we set off for Kalgoorlie. Whilst we were waiting for our flight to be called, I noticed quite a few Desperate Dan figures with large beards, a lot of hair, and large boots.

"They're going to Kalgoorlie," said David. I thought he was joking, but he was right.

Kalgoorlie is a wonderful town. I have to confess that my passion for cowboy and Indian films is no way politically correct. I revel in the ones where the Apache are ravaging and pillaging and staking you out over anthills. When we hit Kalgoorlie, it seemed as if it had just stepped out of the Wild West, and I fully expected John Wayne to mosey up the main street and hitch his horse up outside one of the many bars. It still very much has the air of a frontier town, full of hairy miners and strippers, with the smell of beer wafting out of the open windows of the numerous pubs open twenty-four hours to cater for miners on shift work.

When we arrived we went for a little explore. I noticed a sign saying, "Skimpies to'nite".

"I wonder what skimpies are," I said. "Do you think they are some sort of shellfish?"

"Don't know," said David. "Never heard of them."

A bit further along was another sign: "Hot skimpies to'nite". "Maybe they are going to barbecue them," I mused.

A little bit further still and we saw a blackboard outside a pub: "Red hot skimpies to'nite".

"They must be cooked with chilli," I trilled. It was only when I peered into one of these pubs and saw the barmaid in her bra and pants that I realised "skimpies" meant girls in their undies!

I had, in my ignorance, been a little chary of the accommodation in Kalgoorlie. Visions of outside dunnies with spiders the size of dinner plates waiting to pounce danced in my head. How pleasantly surprised I was. For all its Wild West main street, it is a charming and rather cultured town. We stayed in a delightful hotel which had, until recently, been part of the Mercure chain, and boasted an excellent restaurant.

The first evening we went into dinner. The restaurant was about half full and we were seated at a table which could accommodate four. I was feeling slightly self-conscious as the only woman there among the hairy miners when, all of a sudden, I heard, "Hello, dears. How lovely to see you."

There, seated with us, was Prucel.

"Darling," I said to David, "I think your grandmother is here."

Well, she certainly was! She joined us for dinner every evening and chatted away happily all through the meal. All thoughts of romantic tete-a-tetes hit the deck as most of the conversation consisted of, "Prucel says this, Prucel says that!" At first I think David thought the heat and an excess of excellent Australian wine had got to me, but the more Prucel reminisced, the more he realised I couldn't possibly have known most of the things she was talking about. David was brought up in a Jewish household but, having had a gentile mother, is not Jewish himself. When his grandfather went out, Prucel used to make him secret bacon sandwiches, throwing open all the doors and windows to waft out the smell of frying bacon before Morrie got home.

I had never seen any pictures of David's family until a couple of years after this visit. We were clearing out his late father's flat when we came across a cache of old photos. I pounced on them with glee, rummaging through to find pictures of the young David, and there was a photo of the lovely little lady I had first met in Kalgoorlie.

During our stay, we went looking for the house where David's father was born. We tracked it down; it was an elegant colonial house surrounded by a verandah. The front garden had been lovingly landscaped and white roses blossomed abundantly. We rang the bell. A charming lady of about my age opened the door. When David explained who he was and what we were doing ringing her doorbell at 6 pm on a Sunday evening, she invited us in. The house belonged to her daughter and had been exquisitely and sympathetically restored.

"My daughter is especially fond of the front garden," said the lady. "When they bought the house it was very overgrown, but she worked hard to restore it to its former glory. A friend of hers who is a landscaper said it is probably the garden laid out by the original owners. The roses are certainly very old and my daughter was very keen to preserve them."

That evening at dinner: "Hello, dears. I do hope you liked my garden. I did try to tell you about it in Perth."

Prucel has a habit of popping in unexpectedly. David was telling me one day about some fish she used to cook in a very light batter. Now, I'm a good cook, but my batter has never cut the mustard as far as David is concerned. All of a sudden, there she was.

"You must always use soda water, dear, never still water. It's the soda water that gives it the lightness." And she's right.

When I first came to live in Australia, I found the heat very difficult. We left a snowbound England, shivering at -12 C, to arrive twenty-four hours later in a sweltering +40. The dog, who had been sent under separate cover, didn't stop moulting for six months. After a couple of weeks, we found a sweet little old cottage in a very nice area of Sydney, but unfortunately, without air conditioning. I remember standing in the tiny kitchen, cooking dinner with the sweat running off me, and snivelling with heat and homesickness. Suddenly, I was conscious of a small but feisty presence. It was Prucel. "I know it's difficult, dear," she said, "but take strength from the fact that I managed in Kalgoorlie in more difficult circumstances and a lot more clothes!"

She despairs of my posture and has been known to give me a sharp dig in the middle of my back to make me sit up straight. I had a very embarrassing experience one day while slouching across the main road of the sleepy little Georgian town where we lived in England. Suddenly, I felt a painful jab between my shoulder blades. I let out a shriek and jerked to attention, scattering little old ladies on Zimmer frames to the four winds, and frightening small children. "That's better, dear," she said as I marched into Tesco's with a posture worthy of the Blues and Royals.

Gran and Prucel get on extremely well. There was a certain wariness when they first met, but this quickly dissipated. Now, if they ever appear together, they are hatted and gloved, and dressed as if they are on their way out to afternoon tea. It's a lovely idea to think of them delicately sipping Earl Grey or playing a hand of bridge, gossiping away together.

Move over Grey Owl. Make way for the grannies.

CHAPTER 25

During one of our trips to France, we decided to visit the village of Oradour-Sur-Glane.

During the Second World War, as the Germans were retreating back up through South West France, a group of partisans attacked them and managed to kill quite a few of the Bosch. The Germans found out that the men were from a village called Oradour, and decided to punish the villagers for daring to attack the mighty, albeit retreating, German army. They marched into Oradour and shot every man they could find. They herded the women and children into the church. They set fire to the church, barring the doors and windows to prevent any escape. Afterwards, it emerged that the partisans were from another village also called Oradour, but not Oradour-Sur-Glane.

The original village has been kept unaltered as a monument to those who perished, but a new Oradour has risen from the ashes nearby. This is a pretty little place with a main square full of flowers and a bustling bistro serving good food. The day we went to visit, the sun was shining and the birds were singing lustily. All was well with the world, especially after a good lunch and a glass of wine.

We finished our coffee and embarked on the purpose of our visit - to see the ruins of what I had imagined to be a small village. It was not what I expected. It had been quite a sizeable town and had even had a tram system. We walked through the burnt out streets in eerie silence, both deeply moved by the horrors that had taken place. No birds sang here.

There is a theory that when a traumatic event occurs, such a massive amount of energy is released that the event is somehow imprinted on its surroundings, and that from time to time these imprints become visible again, so what we are seeing is not actually happening, but some ghostly photograph from years gone by.

I'm not sure that I go along with this opinion. To me the spirit world is much too real and, whereas I believe an atmosphere can linger in a place like Oradour, it doesn't explain my experience there.

We walked on through the cobbled streets. Suddenly something tugged at my sleeve. I looked down. There was a dear little girl of about seven, with a cloud of dark curls and enormous brown eyes, wearing a long white cotton nightdress.

"I've lost my mummy," she said in a small, scared voice. "Please, will you help me find my mummy?"

I knelt down beside her.

"When did you last see Mummy?" I asked, dreading the answer. "She made me hide when the bad men came."

I looked up at David. He hadn't seen the child, but obviously knew something was up given that his wife was kneeling down speaking French to thin air. I started to explain, but when I looked round for the little girl again, she had disappeared.

We walked to the church. It was a harrowing experience. I could hear the screams of the dying, and the crackling flames as those poor souls perished. Mothers trying to shield their children from the inferno, and the brave priest who had accompanied them, crying out to Our Lord for salvation. But you know, as dreadful as that was, the one thing that still haunts me about Oradour is that little moppet in her nightie saying, "S'il te plaît, aide-moi trouver maman."

When I was a child and used to go to watch cowboy movies with my father on a Saturday afternoon, life was very simple. You knew who was the goodie and who was the baddie because the baddies always wore black hats.

If only things were the same with the spirit world.

Most of the time, I'm more than happy to share my life with those from another dimension. Apart from my close coterie of spirits, beings such as Christopher and his piano have given me a great deal of pleasure, even though he scared the dinner guests half to death, but there are those "stuck in the astrals" as Mrs. Caesar would say, that I don't particularly want around.

At first, after my husband John died, life was relatively peaceful, but gradually things started to go bump in the night. We didn't actually have objects hurled round the room, but there were unexplained bangings and crashings, shapes seen fleetingly out of the corner of my eye, and dimmer switches seemingly moving of their own volition. Poltergeists often appear in houses where there are young teenage girls, supposedly feeding off adolescent angst. Maybe Lulu's and my emotions after John's death provoked something. Who knows?

It got so bad that I got the house exorcised. Now, this is not as easy as it sounds. I found a vicar who did exorcisms, but I was put through rigorous questioning before he believed I wasn't just a nutter with a vivid imagination. We had three meetings, all of which turned into wide ranging and fascinating theological discussions. Eventually he suggested a Requiem Mass for John. I pointed out that we weren't Catholic, but he said it didn't matter, we should just give his soul some peace.

The day dawned and the vicar duly arrived with a large case. He set up a makeshift altar on the breakfast room table and, from the depths of his capacious bag, produced a candle, a cross, a bell, a Bible, and a flagon of holy water. We went through every room in the house, cloakrooms included, with the vicar sprinkling holy water, ringing his bell and telling any demon to go back whence it came. It really was bell, book, and candle! We then celebrated the Mass for John and I remember hoping the vicar didn't include John in with the demons lurking behind the loo!

This calmed things down for a while, but maybe the spirits weren't good Christians because they did reappear later.

I have mentioned recurring dreams, most of which vanished when I met David. A psychiatrist would probably say that was because he made me secure and fulfilled all my emotional needs, which of course is absolutely true. Nevertheless, there was one dream that refused to go away. It was about a house; a beautiful, light, warm, elegant house full of plants and flowers. In my dream I had hordes of people coming to stay and nowhere to put them. Suddenly, I would remember a lot of extra unused rooms. I would open a locked door, go along a corridor, and find about five more bedrooms with fantastic bathrooms. I would start to get the rooms ready, but always with a feeling of cold unease. There was something menacing about that area of the house, and why had it been so firmly locked up?

When David and I came to view our funny old house in Hampshire for the first time, we virtually bought it on the doorstep. We drove into this lovely Georgian town and turned into a wide street with pastel-painted houses and hanging baskets of flowers. We parked outside the house, went up a couple of wide stone steps worn by footsteps over the centuries, and rang the rather important bell. The minute the door was opened and we looked into the elegant high-ceilinged hall, we were lost. Within a couple of months we moved in.

Every time we went to see the house it was fine, not the slightest hint that anything was wrong. But as soon as we moved in I began to feel things were not as they should be – and that was not just due to the wallpaper in the dining room that made you feel as if you were back in the sixties on LSD. The Cavalier and the young footless boy were fine. They were entitled to be in the house just as much as we were and we all rubbed along together quite happily.

The trouble started with the woodworm man. Having woodworm treated is a very mucky experience in an old house like ours. All the floorboards had to be taken up, revealing literally centuries of dust and dirt, but also revealing something slightly more sinister. The atmosphere of the old house changed. I could feel presences around me. They were not doing anything, just watching and waiting.

I thought they were put out by all the disruption, and assured them it was only temporary, but once normality had been re-established, they still watched and waited.

Before we restored the room where we had found the secret room, it had been a dentist's surgery, and there was only one door to it from the second staircase. Having established that the wall from the main corridor was only a plywood partition, we decided to open it up and put a door in from the passage. The house had originally been two houses, then one, then two again, finally becoming one whole house back in the nineteenth century. Every incarnation had produced a different floor level, and consequently there were three sets of floorboards with quite a large gap in between each.

We pulled at the plywood partition which came down very easily. As it did, there was an almighty whoosh from the exposed floor levels. It was as if a huge vacuum had been released, although, given the amount of roof space, gaps, and draughts, that was impossible.

"Crikey!" said David. "What in the world was that?"

As we looked at each other in slight consternation, we heard a man's deep voice say, "You've summoned me, now make use of me."

What had we done? We hadn't summoned anyone. What had we released from under the floor? Whatever it was, it didn't seem very friendly.

We were both very much aware that imagination can be a very powerful force, although it was a tad coincidental that we heard the same voice. However, we had the room refurbished and put it to the back of our minds.

But the released spirit did seem to liven up the others who became decidedly more active. Whenever I went into the old house, I would feel a distinctly icy chill.

"Sorry, guys," I would say. "Won't be long."

But all this time the watching and waiting continued.

I had lucky escapes. Six weeks after we moved in, the top of a heavy stone bird bath hit me on the heels, missing both Achilles tendons by millimetres. I went into hospital for a simple operation and very nearly died due to a collapsed lung and pneumonia. I got breast cancer, but luckily was diagnosed early. I kept falling over. Mirrors crashed down and missed me or the dog by inches. The atmosphere became more menacing and the dog refused point blank to go anywhere near the back stairs.

The first time I had any inkling that something really serious was afoot was in Australia. On our second trip we had gone out to buy a suitcase, and ended up with a flat in a luxurious new development in Sydney's Central Business District. By the time we went back the following year, the apartment was completed and we moved in. I was like a pig in clover in such a glamorous environment.

One night, getting ready for bed, I was cleaning my teeth in our amazingly sexy bathroom, and feeling very happy with the world. I looked into the mirror. The eyes looking back at me were not mine. Physically there was a resemblance, but what was looking through them was no way me!

I dropped the toothbrush and shot into the living room like a scalded cat. I grabbed David's hands.

"Quick! Pray with me!"

David appeared rather startled, not least because I was foaming at the mouth due to the toothpaste.

"Pray with me! I'm possessed!"

To give him his due, he didn't argue, and we recited the Lord's Prayer together until I had regained control of my soul.

I tried to explain what had happened but, not surprisingly, David found it very hard to believe, putting it down to a trick of the light or a surfeit of Sauvignon. It was only back in England that he realised the truth.

We had had a tiff. Not a row, not a falling out, just a tiff. Suddenly, I started to say the most horrible things to him. I swore dreadfully and a stream of filth poured from my mouth. The colour drained from David's face. I fainted. I came to after a minute or so to find David holding me close. We both knew that wasn't me speaking. David stroked my hair tenderly and said, "I think it's time to get Phil."

Our vicar rejoiced in the name of Phil Collins and was one of the funniest men I have ever met. The Bishop wanted to reward him for all his sterling work and asked him if he would like to go on a course of his own choosing. Phil thought for a moment and then replied that as he had done quite a few courses, could he please go to clown school! His sermons virtually had us rolling in the aisles, but this in no way detracted from his faith nor his compassion. If all vicars were like Phil, churches would be packed to the rafters every Sunday.

We arranged for him to come and give the place the once over. As we were having a cup of tea before starting the tour of the house, I told him about my strange experience. David was with us and said to Phil, "The very scary thing about it was the man's voice."

"What are you talking about?" I asked. To me my voice had sounded normal.

"Well," continued David. "When you were saying all those terrible things, you were speaking in a very deep man's voice, a bit like demons in the movies."

I nearly fainted all over again. I had had no idea, but the thought that I truly had been possessed terrified me.

We talked more about whatever it was that was happening to me. Phil thought that maybe I hadn't always been careful about protecting myself during readings and that somehow a channel had been opened. I thought it was what we had released from under the floor. We prayed and Phil blessed me and gave me a passage from the Bible to read before every reading.

We made our way around the house. Obviously the watchers decided to keep a low profile, because for most of the tour they were not much in evidence, just lurking in the background. We went up the main stairs in the new house, looking into every bedroom and bathroom and then through into the old house. Even the top flat wasn't bad. We came down the back stairs. Phil led the way.

"There is something in the house," he said. "Although I can't feel it too strongly."

"Christ, what was that?" he suddenly exclaimed.

He jumped the last three steps and shot into the library like Road Runner. I swear you could see smoke at his heels.

I ran after him.

"I think you're right," he said. "We need to do something."

I hadn't realised that each diocese had its own exorcist, although he is known by a much more user friendly name. However, both Phil and I got caught up with the Poppy Appeal and Christmas and never got round to the spiritual fumigation. I kept well away from that part of the house and made sure any communicating doors were firmly shut.

David and I found that we were rattling around in such a big house and so we had had it on the market for over a year, but what with the GFC and plunging property prices, we had had no takers for it. Having become resigned to staying put, we were totally taken by surprise when, in late November, we had an offer. We hadn't even bothered to look for anywhere else and so we had to scuttle around quickly.

The weather was awful and poor David, who can't stand the cold, was getting more miserable by the minute. By this time he was wearing so many layers he looked like an onion. He wanted to go home. He wanted the sunshine and warmth of Australia.

And so, in early January, we packed up and left for Australia. It was so cold that the dog's flight couldn't take off and he had to spend five days in super deluxe heated kennels at the airport. The packers couldn't get to us for three days because of snow, but eventually we left -12C and arrived in Sydney to a heatwave of +40C. David's bones were so frozen he couldn't take his jumper off for a couple of days.

Hopefully, we left behind any malign presences and, also hopefully, the new owners of the house have no problems. One thing you can be sure of, whenever I do any psychic work now, I make sure I am very well protected.

CHAPTER 26

People often ask me if animals are included in the spirit world and I am totally convinced they are. I am sure animals understand and feel a lot more than we give them credit for and I see no reason to think that their souls do not continue as do those of humans.

My love affair with animals, especially dogs, started when I was six years old. My father had a distant cousin called Marjorie who had a slightly louche reputation within the family, having married a much older and rather well off gentleman called Harry. One day, Marjorie came to tea sporting a hat elegantly slanted over one eye, a fur tippet, and an inordinate amount of lipstick, and carrying a miniature apricot-coloured poodle who could dance on his hind legs. I was captivated by this little creature and cried buckets when they left.

I was determined to have a poodle and so began a guerilla campaign to get one of my very own. I gradually ground down my parents and it was finally agreed that I would have a poodle for my seventh birthday.

One Sunday, two weeks before my birthday, Gran came pounding down the stairs – a rather startling occurrence given that she was a very large lady – waving aloft the Parish Magazine. It took us a while, having sat her down, fanned her, and given us all hot sweet tea for the shock, but she finally managed to gasp out that there was a notice in the magazine about a home for a dog. An RAF chap was being posted abroad and wanted a good home for his Labrador. Daddy rang the number and that evening the man came round holding the lead of a large black dog with a white star on his chest and four white socks. Skippy and I looked at each other and all thoughts of apricot poodles disappeared. It was instant, mutual love. He was my bosom companion on my solitary only-child adventures, my right hand in the pirate ship, and my patient for doctors and nurses. We were inseparable for twelve years and I mourned him greatly when he died.

Husband John had also had a black lab called Sonny, so we both had a great fondness for large dogs. When we got married, we lived in a flat overlooking Wimbledon Common. After a couple of months of wedded bliss, we both started to miss a canine presence. We decided to get a dog, but couldn't decide what sort. Neither of us wanted a small dog, but a large one was out of the question in a small flat.

We decided on a compromise. Working on the principle that they looked big, but were not tall, we decided on a Basset hound, and so, one cold January day, we trekked off to a house called Mandalay in Old Coulsdon to meet Mrs. Langmead, basset breeder extraordinaire. She was a rather rangy lady with a hairdo reminiscent of Auntie Marjorie's apricot poodle, who travelled the country with a station wagon full

of Bassets, competing in various dog shows. She invited us into her kitchen where she was cooking sausages for her husband's tea, right next to an extremely evil looking pan of dog food. I did hope she wasn't going to muddle them up, especially as the poor man had lost all his hair due to an attack of typhoid caught while serving overseas.

"I'll bring the little chap in," said Mrs. L. She went out of the room and reappeared a few minutes later preceded by a clatter of claws on the wooden floor and a small bundle of fur which promptly trod on its own ear, skidded, and ended up in a heap at my feet. And so Barnaby Basset came into our lives.

We took him home, swathed in a purple bedcover, and installed him in our flat. We had been told that at night we should close him in the kitchen, which happened to be next to our bedroom.

It started as a whimper. "Oh, poor little dog," I said. "I must go to him."

"No," said John. "Leave him. He'll quieten down and go to sleep."

Suddenly there was a dreadful noise, a cross between a lonesome coyote and a soul in torment.

"Whatever was that?" I jumped about three feet in the air.

We crept into the kitchen to find poor little Barnaby cowering in a corner. He had found his voice for the first time and every time he bayed, he scared himself to death! "I think we may have made a mistake," said John.

Barnaby wasn't the easiest dog in the world, not helped by the fact that at six months he was run over outside the flat and very badly injured. He was saved by a super young Australian vet, but needed constant nursing for quite a while. Needless to say, this didn't help with basset training. He was a very intelligent little dog and got to know the sound of the car engine. He didn't start baying until he heard it start up, but he didn't stop baying until he heard it stop! We were blissfully ignorant of this until we got home one night at about 2 am to find our neighbour asleep on a chair in front of our door, waiting to enlighten us!

"That's it!" said John. "You've got to do something about your dog."

I rang the Kennel Club. "Is there somewhere I can send my dog to be trained?" I asked.

"Of course," came the helpful reply. "Ring this lady. She can train anything."

It turned out it was Mrs. Barbara Woodhouse before she became famous.

"Can you train my dog?" I asked. "Course I can. What is it?"

"It's a Basset."

"Save your money, dear. Can't do a thing with hounds."

"But he won't stop barking."

"Very vocal, hounds," she said brusquely, and put the phone down.

I looked at Barnaby who gazed back at me innocently, but with a vague smirk. I guess we both knew who had won that round.

They do say that animals are more sensitive to the spirit world than people. That hasn't always been my experience, but I have certainly seen instances of it.

Barnaby was a French Tricolour Basset. That meant he was small, elegant, and black, brown and white, although John said it should be spelt trickler as bladder control was not Barnaby's strongest asset. Tricolour meant that no matter what colour you were wearing, he'd get you with some shade of dog hair. He also managed very efficiently to cover the sitting room carpet in white hair, and the white bedroom carpet in black hair.

One day, as I was hoovering said white carpet, I heard a distinct growl. I was in shock! That dog had bayed, barked, yelped, whimpered and I swear on occasion, had even laughed at me, but had never before growled. I looked at him. His mouth was drawn back in a snarl and his hackles were up. His gaze was fixed on a spot above the chest of drawers. I watched in amazement as he began to back away, still growling. He slowly reversed out of the bedroom and down the hall to the front door, all the while growling and keeping his eyes firmly fixed on a spot about six feet above the floor. When he reached the front door, he stopped growling and started to whimper and tremble. I cuddled him and soothed him and gradually he calmed down. He had obviously seen something, although I had been completely unaware of anything out of the ordinary. It never happened again, but as far as Barnaby was concerned, there had definitely been something menacing in the bedroom that day.

In 1970, we moved to a town house in Wimbledon. It was built over four floors, linked by an open tread wooden staircase – very smart at that time. The main drawing room took up the whole of the ground floor. In theory, the open tread staircase was wonderful. In practice it meant that tricolour dog hairs cascaded through the gaps and mostly ended up on the sofa. Guests used to leave looking like yetis.

Barnaby had a problem with the stairs. He still had a penchant for treading on his ears and would regularly lose his footing. You would hear his claws clatter on the first couple of treads and then thump, thump,

thump as he tobogganed down the rest on his breast bone to end up in a yelping heap in the hall. This never really seemed to worry him. He would just pick himself up, have a shake, and go on about his basset business. This went on for the whole nine years we lived there.

Now, this next story about Barnaby is by no means psychic nor spiritual but, shall we say, somewhat more corporeal. I would recommend that those of a delicate disposition skip the next couple of pages!

Husband John was very particular about his appearance. Every morning he would select his outfit for the day. He would lay everything, including underwear, out on the bed, and then go and have his shower. Now, Barnaby was very partial to an early morning sock, and although I'm sure he tried his hardest to resist, every morning temptation overcame him and he would pinch one of John's carefully chosen socks.

It was as regular as clockwork. I would hear the water stop running, count up to five, and then hear the dog skittering down the stairs with John, stark naked except for a towel, in hot pursuit. Barnaby would then take refuge under the large round dining room table where he passed a happy few minutes dodging out of John's grasp. Being an extremely intelligent little dog, he quickly realised that if he swallowed the evidence, there would be nothing to incriminate him and he wouldn't get a clout, so he would look you straight in the eye, gulp, and the sock would disappear, only to reappear in some form or another at a later date.

One day, I was taking him up the road for a constitutional when nature called and Barnaby prepared to do what a dog's got to do. Just at that moment, two very genteel ladies came into view.

"What a beautiful Basset," said one of them. "How old is he?"

Now, because he looked like a hush puppy until the day he died, I often used to lie about his age in an effort to excuse his bad manners. As I was pondering what I could get away with, I glanced down at Barnaby to see a sock starting to emerge from his nether regions.

Barnaby was rapidly becoming aware that all was not well in the tail area. He started to strain, but the sock was firmly stuck, half in and half out. He obviously thought that something was attacking him from behind and began to do a whirling dervish act on the end of the lead, baying at the same time.

"Is he alright?" asked one of the old ladies tremulously.

Evidently not from the performance he was kicking up. There was only one thing to do.

"Sit!" I bellowed.

The dog was so taken aback that he sat down immediately. I put the toe of one boot on the offending sock and the other on the offending canine backside, stood on the first and pushed hard at the second. With one mighty yelp Barnaby was free, but the two old ladies were tottering away up the road as fast as they could go.

In 1979 we moved to "the house" - scene of Christopher and the piano. From the moment we set foot inside that house, Barnaby was terrified. He was constantly shaking and became completely incontinent - not the best thing to deal with having a small child and a husband with a kidney transplant. Eventually, as the poor dog got weaker and sicker, the vet said we should have him put down and so, very sadly, we said goodbye to our little Hush Puppy.

It was not the easiest of times as John was extremely ill and I had been told it was only a matter of weeks. Obviously, Lulu didn't know this, but she had been very upset about the death of her dog, and I wanted to make things as smooth as I could for her. A friend told me that a litter of golden retrievers had just been born and I thought a new puppy might help my darling girl.

We first saw Monty when he was a week old. He was tiny and didn't even have his eyes open. Lulu was enchanted. Allegra, the dog breeder, was a friend of a friend, and very long suffering. Nearly every day after school Lulu and co. would ask to see the puppy. Allegra and I would drink tea whilst a gang of kids and six puppies took off down the garden in full cry after a very large and rather unconcerned pet rabbit.

We must have had Monty for about three months when I bumped into the lady who had bought our town house.

"Hello, my dear," she said. "I hear you have a lovely new dog."

"Yes," I replied. "We've got a Goldie."

"We've still got Barnaby," she said matter-of-factly.

"Excuse me?"

"We've still got Barnaby. We often hear him. His claws clatter on the stairs then we hear thump, thump, thump and yelping."

I didn't know what to say. "I'm awfully sorry," I stammered.

"Oh, that's quite alright. We're used to him now."

The dog had evidently gone back to the home he grew up in and where he was happy. I just hope the poor lady didn't get the dog hairs as well.

Monty seemed blissfully unaware of any ghostly presences and spent a very happy doggy existence in the house that had so terrified poor Barnaby. He was a very gregarious dog and didn't like to be parted from his "mummy". Every evening, he'd trot upstairs with me and settle himself on the floor next to the bed, where he would pass the night snoring and doggy dreaming. In fact, the snoring proved very difficult to explain when an American boyfriend called me at 3 am and thought I had another man with me!

By the time I moved into the big beautiful house with John number two, Monty was getting on a bit. The day we moved in, he was a bit reluctant to cross the threshold, but with a great deal of pulling and pushing, we managed to persuade him. Once inside, he made a bolt for the kitchen quarters, which comprised kitchen, pantry, laundry room, and sitting room, and there he stayed for his remaining three years. He was very happy there and used to spend a lot of time lying on a sheepskin in the middle of the kitchen floor. Unfortunately, he and the rug were the same colour, and consequently people were always tripping over him.

We tried countless times to get him through the passage door, but he could not be moved. I felt quite bereft without the snores and doggy dreams and decided enough was enough – Monty could stop being a doggy diva and come upstairs with me. I hitched up his lead and dragged him into the hall as far as the bottom of the stairs. He panicked, snatched the lead from my grasp, and shot to the front door where he lay panting and shivering. He was generally the most docile dog and this was totally out of character.

"Come on, sweetheart. Come to Mummy," I called.

Mont started to run to me, but suddenly, with great force, was thrown backwards, just as if he had cannoned into a glass wall. I looked up the stairs. There was the lady in pink, glaring at me.

"Please let me get him back to the kitchen," I said desperately. Rustling her skirts, she flounced off and the dog crept towards me. We didn't try that one again. It was quite obvious that, in her opinion, dogs were kitchen animals. The strange thing was, when we got Sammy, Mont's replacement, she was fine and let him wander where he pleased. Perhaps the fact that she had known him from a baby had something to do with it.

Everyone has a special dog in their lives, and mine was Sammy. Another Goldie, he had the sweetest nature and I loved him dearly. In fact, David said that when we got married and "my car/your car" became "our car", the very last thing to become "ours" was the dog. I used to feel a bit silly taking him to the vet. We would await our turn. The nurse would come out and call "Sammy Samuel" at which point I always felt compelled to explain to the assembled company that I had the dog before I had the name!

Sammy understood every word I said to him. John and I took him for a walk on Wimbledon Common. We came to a crossroads and I said, "Left hand down a bit, number one". (Those of you old enough to remember The Navy Lark will appreciate this.)

"Oh, that's right," said John stroppily. "Single words of command. How do you ever expect that dog to obey? Single words of command."

Mid rant, the dog turned left! Extra doggy treats that night!

Sammy also liked a brand of dog food called Scout, and on the tin was printed, "For super heroes." Sometimes I would put his food down and say, "What do super heroes do?" The dog would sit and look at me, drooling buckets until I gave the OK, at which point he would launch himself at his bowl. Can you imagine my surprise when I absentmindedly said to Sammy's successor, Sydney, who was then aged six months and voracious, "What do super heroes do?" to see the puppy sit down, look at me, and wait for the Okay? He had never been taught that in his young life.

Over the years, we have also had a couple of cats deign to share our lives. Neither husband John nor I had ever had cats, in spite of Gran's attempt with the half crown, but two things persuaded us. One dinner time, Lulu, who was the prettiest little girl, looked at us, big brown eyes swimming with tears. "Other people have brothers and sisters," she said. "I haven't got anyone at all and I do feel lonely."

The guilt kicked in big time. John and I looked at each other. Another baby would not have been an easy answer given his state of health. "But," continued our little moppet sweetly, "if I had a little pussycat, I wouldn't be lonely." This sounded a much better bet, but John was still unconvinced.

The next time my mother came to visit, we told her the story.

"If you get a cat, I'm never coming to this house again," she proclaimed.

The minute we closed the front door behind her, John turned to me. "That's it. Get the child a cat," he said.

And so began the pussycat quest.

My friend AnneMarie knew a French family who were relocating from Kensington to New York and were looking for a home for their cat. Madame came to interview us and to see if our house was good enough for her pampered pussycat. Luckily, I had had the presence of mind to send Barnaby Basset to kennels for the weekend. She arrived with Gregoire, an immaculate black and white cat, complete with red velvet collar and that rather disdainful look some Frenchmen have, as if they have a slightly odd odour under their noses.

"'E eats a leetle chopped livaire and a leetle feesh," she said. I thought of the tins of Whiskas waiting in the cupboard. "'E sits on zee draining board while I do zee ironing," she continued, "and sometimes 'e does pipi in zee bath" she trilled joyfully. Gregoire and I eyeballed each other.

"Pussycat," I thought, *"your life is about to change!"*

We evidently passed the test and Gregoire moved in. He had never been outside, having lived in a flat behind the fridge with a rabbit, and his paws were still pink. I dutifully kept him in for a couple of days and then accompanied him into the garden, much to the astonishment of the neighbours, speaking to him in French as he hadn't yet begun to understand English. Suddenly, he shot through a hole in the fence and disappeared. I called and called to no avail. I waved juicy bits of meat through the hole. Rien! I called AnneMarie.

"Don't let that woman come and say goodbye to the cat."

"Why ever not?

"Because I've lost him." "Already?"

"I think he's doing The Longest Journey back to Kensington," I said. "By the way, is Gregoire a common name for a cat in France?"

"God, no! First time I've ever heard a cat called that."

Three days later he reappeared, dusty, cobweb covered, collar on the skew, and a bit of an ear missing, but looking distinctly pleased with himself. He had discovered the great outdoors and never looked back.

He was fine living in the house with an aged basset, but when we got the new puppy, he thought this beyond the pale and left home for seven years, returning only for food and the odd nap in front of the fire. He decided that life with my friend Annica across the road was much nicer. She ran an ordered, tranquil home, and fed him special little bowls of prawns, and he loved her dearly.

Eventually Annica and her family went back to Sweden and an Italian family moved in. As I speak Italian, I took it upon myself to invite the lady of the house for coffee along with another Italian girl who lived in the road. The signora's command of English was limited and I thought it would make her feel more at home to be able to speak to someone in her own language. Early one morning, I awoke to the sound of the doorbell ringing furiously. I shot downstairs and flung open the front door to find my new neighbour in hysterics.

"Whatever's the matter?" I asked.

"Mafiosi, mafiosi," she sobbed. "The mafia are after us."

"I don't think we have a lot of mafiosi in Wimbledon," I tried to comfort her. "What makes you think that?"

"The bodies," she answered dramatically.

"What bodies?"

"I came out this morning to find six headless mice on my doorstep. It is a sign!"

Out of the corner of my eye, I caught sight of the guilty party slinking across the lawn, looking slightly sheepish. Obviously, he hadn't realised Annica had left and was still bringing her presents!

Gregoire was a terrible thief and a reprobate, but nobody seemed to hold it against him. Any open door was an invitation, and he would just stroll in and help himself to any tasty morsel he could find. He had Frank's steak that was defrosting for his supper, and a couple of brace of pheasant that Hans de Gier had proudly bagged. All anyone ever said was, "Oh, it's only Gregoire. He must have been hungry," and he never got into trouble. He was the original Teflon cat. However, some neighbours further up the road returned home after a foreign posting. The husband was frightfully precious, and in the fifties any film studio would have cast him as "upper class twit". I was being talked at by him at a drink's party when he said, "I wish I knew who the black and white cat belongs to."

"Oh, that's me" I simpered, expecting paeans of praise to be heaped on furry ears. "Well, it keeps pooing in my heathers!"

"Oh dear," I murmured.

"I've even planted holly, but it doesn't seem to deter him."

Before I could stop myself, out came the reply, "Well, he is French you know!"

Over the years, Gregs had managed to get quite a good grasp of English, but the strange thing was that when he was old and dying and in quite a lot of distress, he was very comforted if I spoke French to him.

I am convinced that animals have a depth of feeling and comprehension beyond that which we attribute to them. I have heard before that animals will pay their respects to dead or dying members of their clan, and I did in fact witness this myself.

David and I were on our way back from a business trip, having left Sammy with a good friend. It was a lovely day in South West France and the road was clear. I was jittery.

"What's the matter?" asked David.

"I don't know. I just know that we have to be on that plane."

"Don't be daft, we've got ages," he replied.

Suddenly, just outside Limoges, the traffic came to a standstill. Nothing was moving. I panicked.

"Don't worry," said David. "Even if the worst comes to the worst, we can go back to the flat and get a plane tomorrow."

I panicked even more.

"No, no, we *must* be on this plane," I insisted.

David shot off the motorway, thinking we would be quicker going through the town. Unfortunately, the airport wasn't signposted and everyone we asked gave us conflicting directions. Eventually, with me in an uncommon state of near hysteria, we made the plane with minutes to spare.

When we landed, I turned on my phone to find a message from my friend saying that she had dropped Sammy off at the house and to let her know if we were delayed.

We got back home to find Sammy dying. He had been fine when Margaret dropped him off, but a valve had suddenly ruptured in his heart. He had dragged himself to the door, waiting for us to come home. David immediately called the vet and I sat on the doormat, cradling Sammy's head. Our little cat, Penny, had run up when she heard us arrive. When she saw Sammy, she jumped over me and licked his face, then settled down curled up against my knees. The vet arrived. She was a sweet South African girl who knew Sammy well. "I'm afraid it's time," she said. Because his pulse was very weak, she had to inject straight into his heart, which takes longer to take effect.

I knelt with my head on Sammy's, tears streaming down my cheeks, the cat in the crook of my knees. "He's gone," said the vet gently. I raised my head. Penny got to her feet. She walked up to Sammy, stopped, and bowed her head. She stayed there for a couple of minutes, head still bowed, and then walked backwards out of the door and sat down in the garden, watching him. "I've never seen anything like that," said the vet.

Penny had definitely been paying her last respects to her friend.

To end this chapter on a chirpier note, I have a friend who is an animal communicator. People consult her about live animals, lost animals, and dead animals, and she has done a lot of work internationally with different zoos. She is a lovely lady, but does have a tendency to take herself a little seriously from time to time.

Anyway, Jane came down for the weekend and another friend, Valerie, came to have supper with us. During dinner, when I came back from the kitchen, Valerie asked me if Sammy had had his dinner.

"Hours ago," I replied, slightly puzzled.

Later Valerie explained. Whilst I was in the kitchen, Jane had said to her, "I'm very worried about Sam."

"Why's that?" asked Valerie, looking at the dog spark out on the carpet. "He's telling me that he's very distressed."

Valerie eyed the sleeping dog. "Why's that?"

"He's telling me that he's starving and they haven't fed him."

The next day the three of us were involved in some sort of psychic fair. At about 6 pm we staggered back to my house for a glass of wine. I looked down at my faithful hound sitting by my side.

"Who was a naughty boy yesterday?" I asked. His ears slid down his head and he looked at me mournfully.

"Who told Auntie Jane porky pies?"

Valerie spluttered into her wine. The dog's ears slid further down his head.

"Who said he hadn't had his dinner when he had?"

Jane didn't even have the grace to blush. Without twitching a whisker, she replied, "Oh, they do that, you know? They tell fibs to get attention."

CHAPTER 27

M ost psychics use some sort of "prop", be it cards, a crystal ball, holding a personal object, or whatever they like to use. This is simply to channel messages. It is a pretty party trick and all too easy to pick up someone's thoughts. For example, if someone comes to see me who is madly in love with a man called Fred, she will be hoping against hope that I will tell her Fred worships the ground on which she walks. It would be quite simple to tell her that there was someone called Fred in her life, at which point she would be totally amazed, think I was wonderful and believe anything I went on to tell her.

In order to avoid that, I use cards as a channel. I am not a tarot reader as such, and couldn't tell you what most of the cards mean. As I look at them, different details seem to become magnified. I focus on these and start to get information. It is almost like having one of those little mikes in my ear, like the newscasters have.

There are three types of clairvoyance. The first category is clairvoyant, which means the medium can see spirits usually as clearly as if they are there in the flesh. The second category is clairaudient, which means that psychics can hear and distinguish between voices. The third is clairsentient, which is what I think I am. It means feeling things clearly, and I feel presences rather than see or hear them. I can often describe a spirit's appearance in detail or know whether the voice talking to me is young or old, male or female, but I don't see and hear as I do normally.

I can't be more specific than to tell you that I see with an inner eye and hear with an inner ear.

When I do a reading, I'm not really aware of anything being different from having an ordinary chat, but my clients tell me it is a stream of consciousness. Once the reading is over, I tend not to remember what I've just said. I can only think that Gran talks through me bypassing the brain. People ring me up and say, "You know what you told me?"

"No."

"Well, it all happened exactly as you said."

"Good God, did it really?" I reply in astonishment. I suppose I shouldn't really say that. What I should say is, "Well, of course it did," but to be honest, it still takes me by surprise.

I don't have any rituals before I start a reading. I don't light candles or cleanse the room with crystals and smudge sticks - not because I think there is anything wrong with this, but just because I don't really know what I'm doing. Most other tarot readers I know keep their cards swathed in silk, which they reverentially and ritualistically unwrap at the start of a session. Mine are in a Tesco's bag. I spend a few minutes before each reading asking for God's help, but that's all. Maybe I should do more, but it seems to work for me.

I would just like to clarify one point. There is a general assumption that clairvoyance excludes a belief in God and that we conform to some sort of white witchery, dancing naked in the dew on certain days – a very scary thought at my age and weight! Most good clairvoyants – and I know how many charlatans there are out there – do not believe they can do this work without God's help, guidance, and protection, and I for one have an extremely strong faith.

My work has evolved over the years. When I first moved to Hampshire, it was a long way for clients to come down from London. I remember one who made the trek, a stunningly beautiful girl, also called Allie, who rang me from her car on her way down to see me.

"Where am I?"

"I don't know, where do you think you are?"

"I've just passed a signpost saying Cuckoo's Corner. I think I'm going bloody cuckoo!"

Another client in North London was very upset.

"Can't you come up to London to do readings?" she asked plaintively. As I was pointing out the impracticalities of this suggestion, I suddenly had an idea.

"We could try a telephone reading, "I suggested. "Let's see if it works and obviously, if it doesn't, there's no charge."

We set a date. At the appointed hour I was sitting by the phone, cards cleared and shuffled. When she rang, I shuffled them again until she told me to stop. I then cut them into three, just like a client would do in person, and got her to choose the pile. I lay the spread down and carried on normally. To the utter amazement of us both, it worked! Now I would say that more than half the readings I do are over the phone. I have quite a few clients in Canada and in France, Germany and Zimbabwe, as well as all over the British Isles. I don't take credit cards; I trust them to send a cheque if they are happy with the reading. I must say that in eleven years, I have only had one lady who didn't honour her debt.

I also do readings in French. Now, one would suppose that being a trained linguist, this would not be difficult, but it does depend where I am. If I am actually in France, there is no problem, although I find myself addressing close friends with the formal "vous" rather than the more intimate "tu" that I would normally use. Doing a phone reading from England is another matter. I stutter and stammer and search for words. I would give myself a B- at GCSE. I can only put it down to the fact that different guides pop in. I must have a French guide in France but a linguistically challenged one over here!

I must digress here for a moment. I did a reading for an English girl who had lived in Rome for some time and who had an Italian boyfriend. I got a very strong vision of a harbour at night. There were quite a few furtive looking men standing around and I got the impression of some sort of contraband being smuggled in. Suddenly there was the sound of gunfire. As I relayed the message, the girl looked frightened. Her boyfriend was some sort of crook with mafia connections and, whereas she didn't know exactly what he was involved in, she knew there were a few dodgy deals cooking. I certainly didn't want to know any more but I told her she must tell her boyfriend what had happened. I don't know what transpired and I don't know if the Gunfight at the OK Harbour took place, but the next time I saw her she told me that her boyfriend had been gobsmacked and just kept repeating, "Questa donna è una strega!" That woman's a witch!

Sometimes people call me to make an appointment for themselves and a friend. When I explain that I would be delighted to see them one after another, they usually tell me that it's not a problem having the friend in the room, they will tell each other everything anyway. The problem is not for them, it's for me – or rather Gran. The only time it does work is if the couple is extremely close. Whenever I have a reading, there is always a lot of stuff about David, but then I guess we are joined at the hip.

I had two sisters who used to come to me. They were Greek and could have not have been more different. One was studious, quietly attractive, and charming, although rather shy. The other was a different kettle of fish completely. Stylish, elegant, beautifully coiffed, and rich as Croesus having married into a very wealthy family. She was the most arrogant woman I have ever met. She would ring me and demand a reading there and then. If I told her I was already booked, she would tell me to cancel the existing client as she had come all the way from Athens. She didn't exactly say she was more important than the mere peasant booked in, but the implication was there.

One day she informed me she was coming round with her sister. I asked the sister if she would wait in another room, but madam was having none of it.

"No, she stays," she commanded.

At least she didn't tell us both to sit!

I started the reading.

"That is wrong!" said my prima donna imperiously.

I was surprised. I was only passing on what Gran was telling me, but we are all fallible, even in the spirit world. I continued the reading.

"What are you talking about? You are stupid today."

By this time Gran and I were having difficulty keeping calm.

"I am wasting my time. Nothing you say has any relevance to me."

Then a small voice next to her piped up, "Actually it all relates to me."

Gran was picking up on her sister. Madam was well miffed, having always been used to being top cat. She flounced out and, thank goodness, never came back, although I continued to read for her sister until I left London.

Readings somehow seem to tailor themselves to the individual. I had one client who was an extremely successful business woman. She was a close friend and I probably knew more about her love life than anyone apart from the two active participants. However, she played her business cards very close to her chest, which is possibly why she was so successful. Whenever she had a reading, it was definitely a game of two halves. When we were talking about her boyfriend, everything was out in the open, no holds barred, but when we started to talk about money, I didn't have a clue what was going on. Guarded messages came through that I didn't understand at all. Veiled advice about business deals was couched in coded terms. I never understood a word but Rene was always happy and said I helped her a lot. It seems that spirit could give the advice she wanted in terms only she would understand.

When I was in London especially, word used to spread like wildfire. One person, usually a young woman, would come to see me then go back to her office and tell all her friends and colleagues, who would in turn book a reading. I used to say I could set up a tent in the atrium of Salomon Brothers as so many of my clients worked there. They were all beautiful, bright young ladies, and I always looked forward to their visits.

One day one of them rang me to say her mother was coming to London and would like a reading. We duly fixed a date and along they trotted. Mother was a very pleasant but no nonsense lady from

Lancashire. I settled daughter down with a coffee and a copy of Vogue, and whisked Mother into my parlour. She never said a single word during the entire hour apart from an occasional grunt. Now, I definitely do not want clients to feed me information, but I do like to know I'm properly tuned in. There is nothing worse than going to see a clairvoyant who spouts irrelevant rubbish at you and then charges you money, saying, "I hope I've helped you, dear." Anyway, Mum wasn't giving anything away at all. I did the reading, trusting that at least Gran knew what she was doing even if I didn't.

When we finished, Mum fixed me with a beaming smile. "Thank you," she said. "That was so helpful and amazingly accurate." I should have trusted Gran more!

For me, the most difficult readings are those I do for friends or clients I know well. The temptation is to fit information that I'm being given into their situation because I'm so familiar with their lives. Just before I met John number two I had a tarot reading from Little Sue. I was going out with Roger at the time. "In September, Roger will be making your heart beat fast," she said, knowing that Roger was my boyfriend. By this time Rog and I were on Act Four of what had, over the years, settled into a comfortable relationship. We adored each other but were more best friends than anything else, and I couldn't imagine the excitement ahead. She was right. In September my heart was going like the clappers, but for John. She had just made the assumption that it was Roger.

I know some of my clients get a bit cheesed off with me because I won't be pinned down to identities. After all, if someone comes to me having trouble with her husband and I see The Lovers some way ahead, it's not up to me to tell her to leave the old man as there's a handsome young toy boy on the horizon. It could be someone new, but it could just as easily be that she and her husband will sort out their problems and be happy again. Nonetheless, I am often given clues about appearance, personality, or work which tends to point us in the right direction.

No matter how well I know my "victim", I'm usually given some pointer that I'm picking up for them. For example, best friend, Sarah, came to see me. Now, Sarah and I know absolutely everything about each other, so no surprises there. I started the reading, but I already knew all the information I was being given. How did I know that I was tuned in and on the right path? Suddenly I got a picture of an old man.

"Was there anyone who had bad feet?" I asked.

Sarah looked at me as if I'd gone mad. "I don't know what you're talking about," she said.

"I've got an old man here who was always complaining about his feet. Everyone used to laugh at him about them." Still no flicker of recognition. *"Oh well,"* I thought. *"Can't win 'em all."*

A couple of hours later Sarah rang.

"I've just been telling Mum what you said. You were right. Old Uncle Jim used to come to us for Christmas and he was always going on about his feet. It was a family joke. I'd forgotten all about it." Sometimes spirit has to tell you very obscure things to let you know you are on the right track.

CHAPTER 28

After husband John died, and just as I was starting to see things, friends took me out for dinner. They were the parents of one of Lulu's best friends and had been very supportive both during John's illness and after he died. The conversation turned to the spirit world. To my amazement, Tom, the husband, was fascinated. It transpired he had been seeing things for years but had thought he was going mad. Katie, the wife, didn't have time for "any of that nonsense" and thought we were both quite eccentric. Anyway, we arranged for Tom to come round one evening to talk more about this.

The house I lived in then had a breakfast room with an archway leading into the kitchen. Tom and I were sitting at the table in the breakfast room when I noticed his gaze was transfixed on the archway.

"What is it?" I asked.

"I can see John standing there so clearly," said Tom. They had been very good friends. "But he's wearing the most dreadful suit I've ever seen, all shiny and green and purple. Not the sort of thing John would wear at all."

My first husband had been incredibly well turned out – cashmere sweaters, shirts from Jermyn Street, bespoke suits – but when I first met him he had the most appalling suit. He had had it made by an Italian tailor somewhere in Soho and it made him look like a mafia don. It was green and purple shot silk. Needless to say, one of the first things I did when we got back from our honeymoon was to smuggle the offending item off to Oxfam. Tom had only ever seen John in his elegant days, and the fact that John had appeared to him wearing something so completely out of character showed Tom that he really was seeing him and not imagining it.

Spirits do sometimes have odd ways of making their presence felt. Now, I can't abide the smell of a perfume called Youth Dew. I'm awfully sorry, Estee Lauder. I love your face creams and cover myself in so much of your wonderful body lotion that I go to bed as slippery as a cake of wet soap, but Youth Dew makes me feel as sick as a dog. It is an extremely distinctive smell and you certainly can't mistake it, but if I am ever really down, or scared, or worried, there will be an incredibly strong odour of Youth Dew and I know everything will be alright.

It's happened whilst David has been with me and he can't smell anything, whereas I am coughing and covering my nose with my hankie. Conversely, he often gets the smell of gardenia which, unfortunately, I don't as it is my favourite flower.

One thing I am very preoccupied with in readings is timing, especially for events that have already happened. People have asked what the point is of telling you what you already know, but if I pick up stuff about you that you know to be true, chances are the things I tell you for the future will also come true. If I pick up a past occurrence and I can pinpoint its timing to so many weeks or months, or even years, ago, then it does give a client confidence.

It's not easy to give accurate timings for the future. Time on the other side does not seem to be as we know it. I remember at school, when I was doing my French A-Level, we studied a book called *La Machine Infernale* by Jean Cocteau. It is a fabulous book and I would thoroughly recommend it. Actually, it must be a fabulous book if it survived the teachings of Miss Syvret and I still like it! It is the story of Oedipus, and there is one scene where Oedipus meets the Sphinx who is rampaging around the neighbourhood causing mayhem. In the book, the Sphinx takes the form of a beautiful young girl and she and Oedipus have a long conversation in which she tells him, "Le temps des hommes est de l'éternité plié. Pour nous il n'existe plus." "The time of man is folded in eternity. It no longer exists for us." When I first read it, it struck me as apposite, but over the years, it has taken on a greater importance. People ask me how the spirit world can see the future. My personal view is that the two worlds are like parallel trains travelling at different speeds. Our train trundles along at more or less the same pace, but the spirit train can speed up or slow down. Occasionally the two pull alongside each other and we get information as the doors slide open.

The one thing I can't stress enough is that we always have free will. Readings are not carved in stone and I don't have much truck with the Jansenist idea of pre- destination. My lovely cousin Jill says that readings are like a weather forecast. If rain is predicted, you take your umbrella. I think this is a good way of putting it. If you see a difficult patch coming up, well, forewarned is forearmed, but if the future looks rosy, you can milk it for all it's worth.

I also think clairvoyants have a great responsibility towards their clients. People usually consult us, for the first time at least, because they are distressed or unhappy. I'm not counting here what I call the Diana and Fergie syndrome, that is folk who bat from one psychic to another hoping to get the answer that suits them. I'm talking about people who genuinely need help for one reason or another. What I try to do is help people solve their own problems by seeing things more clearly. If you think about it, the word clairvoyant means seeing clearly, and I truly believe that if someone distanced from your life picks up a problem that is troubling you, it gives you a new perspective on things. There is also a fine line to be drawn between giving hope and giving false hope. I am often asked if I give bad news as well as good. The answer is that I pass on what I'm given, but in this way troubles can be avoided or dealt with, for example getting a health check before a problem gets serious. If I had been Princess Diana's clairvoyant, I'm sure I wouldn't have foreseen her death, but maybe I would have told her Paris wasn't such a hot idea, as I think was the case with her own very talented clairvoyant.

I must make it clear here and now that I never see death in the cards. The death card does not mean death, it means change and new beginnings, and I usually see it as very positive. (That being said that, I did see death once but in a very positive fashion. Anyway, that's for the next chapter. That should make you read on – almost as much of a cliffhanger as who killed JR.) As I said before, events are not all predestined, and I think psychics who foretell death are totally irresponsible. You can see periods of illness or danger. Maybe you can see the need to sort out your affairs, but to tell someone when they are going to die? Never!

When the mother of one of my best friends hit fifty-eight she got as drunk as a skunk at her birthday party. The next morning, as she was nursing her poor sore head and we were dispensing coffee and aspirin, we gently asked why she had gotten so pissed. She was not normally a toper.

"It's really silly," she said. "It was relief. When I was a young woman, I saw a clairvoyant who told me I was going to die when I was fifty-seven. I was so relieved when I made it to fifty-eight. I had been terrified for the whole year."

The poor woman had spent the last thirty years thinking she was not going to see her grandchildren grow. In fact, she lived a full and happy life until her late seventies.

To my mind, it's totally irresponsible to tell people things like that and I have often had to undo such damage. One of my clients – the one who brought her mum to see me – rang me in tears.

"I need to see you immediately."

"Whatever's wrong?" I was concerned. This wasn't like her. She was usually a phlegmatic northern lass.

"I don't know how to tell you. I feel really embarrassed. God, what was coming? "I went to see another clairvoyant."

Well, that was okay. In fact, I often encourage clients to see other psychics occasionally just in case I'm getting a bit stale.

"She told me I was going to die very soon."

That was serious. She came straight over and we did a reading. Nothing about death at all. The only thing to do with health was a mild warning about sore throats! She went home comforted, but if I had ever got my hands on that other woman, I don't think I would have been responsible for my actions.

How often should one have a reading? This is entirely subjective. Some people are very organised and make appointments regularly every six months or every year. Others just ring when they feel they need it. I don't think there are any set rules about timing, just follow your instincts.

I have been reading for about fifteen years for a fabulous lady called Nicole. She has had a hard life but is unfailingly cheerful and I look forward to her visits. She was going through a traumatic time and came to see me. We did the reading and she went away feeling much happier about things. Three weeks later she rang. "I need to come back."

"No you don't. You've only just been to see me."

"I do. Everything you said has happened already. I need to know what's next." So back she came. This happened about half a dozen times in quick succession and I suggested she should maybe move in for a while! It seemed that God had pushed the fast forward button and things were unravelling at a rate of knots. Just as suddenly, it all calmed down and she didn't need a reading for another year.

I'm often asked if I get tired after readings. Generally, the answer is no; I feel energised. However, it does depend a little on the energy of the person I'm reading for. I don't mean sadness, state of mind or even despair, I mean their basic internal energy. I had one lady in Wimbledon who I found very difficult. I met her at a dinner party in the seventies, and when I first saw her, I thought she was the most stunning woman I had ever seen. She also spoke five languages and ran a very successful business. However, when I started to read for her, she had gone through five husbands and was getting a bit past her sell by date. She was the most demanding client I have ever had and, without fail, after every session, I would take to my bed with a migraine.

I did have a wonderful Irish clan who used to invade me periodically. I use the word clan advisedly because there were an awful lot of them and I never quite worked out who belonged to whom. They used to arrive en masse. I don't remember how they found me in the first place. One of them booked a reading and, when I opened the door to him, I found three others on the doorstep, including a little old lady. I settled them down with cups of tea and went in with my client who was carrying a huge ghetto blaster with enormous pink, blue, mauve, and yellow buttons. My client set it up to record the session.

"That's a fine machine," I said.

"Yes," he replied in an accent that definitely kissed the Blarney Stone. "It belongs to the old lady."

"Really," I murmured, thinking it looked more like the sort of thing some cool dude would be toting in Brixton.

"Yes, she listens to Max Bygraves on it!"

The reading must have been a success because my number of Irish clients increased rapidly and dramatically, but they continued to visit in groups. One day, a new, previously unseen lot arrived complete with ghetto blaster. While serving the ubiquitous cups of tea, I innocently enquired, "You know Mrs. O'Flannagan, don't you?" The effect was startling.

"They said you were amazing! How did you know that? We never said how we got your number. You really must have the sight."

Dear reader, heaven forgive me, for an instant I was tempted, but just as I was about to break into a small, self-deprecating smile, conscience got the better of me and I had to confess it was the Max Bygraves boom machine that had given the game away.

I've already talked about using different channels to communicate with the spirit world, but I found another way almost by accident. After the adventure with Allie and the Ouija board, I confessed our sins to Mrs. Butterfield. She clucked and ruffled her feathers in disapproval.

"It's really hard for your gran to contact you like that," she said sternly. "She's got a long way to come down through the astrals (those pesky astrals again!) and she gets very tired. If you want to talk to her, write to her."

This was a new one. Where did I address the envelope? Gran, c/o Heaven via the Pearly Gates? What stamp would it need? Must be more than to Australia.

Mrs. B brushed aside my frivolous queries. "Just the pen on the paper and call her. She'll write to you."

I went home feeling very sceptical about the whole business. When Lulu had gone to bed, feeling rather silly, I got out my notepad and pen. "Okay, Gran, if you are here, please let me know." I waited for a couple of minutes and just as I was thinking what a waste of time it was, the pen started to move! At first it looked as if a spider had fallen into an inkwell and then crawled over the page, but gradually it became clearer and, what's more, recognisable as Gran's handwriting! Was I going mad? Had I got some sort of primordial memory of Gran's writing that the inner recesses of my brain were now reproducing? I don't think so. I have continued to communicate in this way over the years and have been given valuable advice and comfort. Sometimes the writing is Gran's, sometimes husband John's, and sometimes even my lovely, lovely friend Annie's, whose writing was always a joke among her friends. I have kept letters from all three and it is definitely their writing. I have even tried, as a test, balancing the pen between my thumb and forefinger rather than holding it and, although the writing is much more laboured, it still works. Right again, Mrs. B!

CHAPTER 29

Over the course of the years I have met some truly wonderful people. My clients have come in all shapes and sizes, with personalities covering the whole spectrum. There are some that stand out in my memory more than others, and some with whose lives I have become very involved. But there are some people who touch your life, no matter how briefly, and light it up so that you treasure them forever.

Now, who takes the trouble to re-record their voice message everyday so you are greeted with, "Happy Monday," or "Happy Tuesday," or whatever the day may be? Well, Annie Pelligrini did. Lovely, blonde, bubbly, bouncy Annie, so full of life and with such an interest in everyone and everything around her. She was a social worker in Norfolk and campaigned tirelessly for the aged. She was irreverent, beautiful, and glamorous, and to this day I can't wear hold up stockings without the memory of Annie striding purposefully into a high level meeting, her stockings gracefully sliding down to her ankles.

Annie was a giver. She kept very quiet about it, but had worked with Mother Teresa in Calcutta, and with Native Americans. She was truly psychic and worked with stones. I don't know how she did it, but her readings were amazingly accurate. I still keep a couple of my "Annie stones" on my bedside table.

She thought she was diabetic and put her increasing tiredness down to her blood sugar levels. When she was eventually diagnosed with pancreatic cancer, it was too late to do anything about it.

She faced her mortality with courage, dignity, and a great sense of humour. Who of her friends can forget Annie going to an oncologist's appointment and realising she wasn't wearing any knickers? He came in to find her wearing the blanket like a giant nappy.

Her friend Heather was a star. She supported Annie, went with her for hospital appointments, held her hand, and was always there for her. She also kept Annie's hordes of friends informed about her progress.

Annie loved my Golden Retriever, Sam, and whenever we spoke on the phone, I would put Sammy on to talk to Auntie Annie. The dog would bark at the command "speak" but didn't need to be told when he heard Annie's voice, and would woof away happily.

I spoke to her the day before she died. She sounded a bit weak, but cheerful as always.

"Let me speak to Sammy," she said.

I put the phone by the dog's ear. Nothing. "Speak to Auntie Annie," I said.

Nothing.

"Sammy, speak!" I commanded.

He had never disobeyed this before. We could not get that dog to bark. He looked at me sorrowfully. I am sure that somehow he realised it would be the last time we heard her dear voice.

The next day, Annie died.

Heather, who was quite sceptical about the afterlife, sent us all one last email. She was driving home from the hospice when, suddenly, as clear as a bell, she heard Annie say, "Yippee! It's fantastic! I'm flying with the angels."

I bet she is still flying with those angels and giving them a rare old time. She always said that she didn't want to be remembered as a social worker, but for her work with stones.

Dear Annie, the Stone Lady, those of us whose lives you touched still love you and miss you. Oh! And by the way, we still gossip about you!

It is through Annie that I have a wonderful friend in Toronto called Diana. I have never met her but she and her daughter have the most charming, warmest voices I have ever heard. It's like being hugged down the phone. I have been reading for her for about ten years and I always saw a lovely man coming into her life. Readings unfailingly went along the same lines. We would deal with any matters that needed sorting out and then I would end up by saying, "There's a lovely man coming into your life. You will meet him unexpectedly through friends and it will be instant attraction on both sides."

"You always say that." The gorgeous voice would laugh sceptically.

This went on for about six years. One day, as I put a spread down for her, I reeled back.

"Oh my God," I squeaked. "It's happened. He's here!"

Diana was in a bubble. It had happened just as I had said. A group of friends had come to visit and had brought the lovely man with them. Diana had opened the door, they had looked into each other's eyes, and had both fallen instantly in love.

"I told you so!" I cackled gleefully. "I told you so!"

I have a really nice client in Edinburgh called Christine who has been sort of divorced for years. Things are complicated because she and her almost ex-husband still run a business together. She has a very kind heart and was loathe to make a complete break as she was worried what would become of him without her. I have been telling her for ages that he is not at all vulnerable, in fact just the opposite. I told her to check the accounts very carefully, but she told me there was no way he would do anything like that. She rang me.

"You were right! The bastard! He's been milking the firm's account for ages. I took your advice and started checking. Thank God I found out now before he cleared me out."

"I told you so," I said, so pleased I had been able to help her.

People sometimes contact me in mysterious ways. Susan came to me when she was very unhappy. She had been at the mercy of a cruel, domineering husband who for years had systematically tried to destroy her. This lovely, intelligent, witty woman had been reduced to a timid little shadow. She had popped into a friend's house for coffee. They were in the kitchen and her friend moved a pile of papers off the table. Out fell my card. The friend picked it up.

"Heavens!" she said. "What's that doing here? I didn't even remember I had it. I met this woman at a party about six months ago and asked her for her card."

Susan picked it up. She had never been to a clairvoyant before but felt an urgent need to contact me.

When I first met her, she was so shy and scared, and spoke in such a soft voice that it was difficult to hear what she said. As the reading went on, Gran and I were getting angrier by the minute. I have no trouble accepting that in the break-up of any relationship there is usually blame on both sides, but this was different. What gave anyone the right to treat another person so badly? Gran and her cronies waded in. They stressed that she must get good legal advice, but more importantly, they told her that her life without this monster wouldn't be as awful as he had told her it would be - quite the contrary in fact.

She came to see me a few times and spirit worked very hard. The third time she came, I happened to be standing outside my front door. I looked up the street and saw her skipping down the road, radiating confidence and with a beaming smile on her pretty face. I was so happy to see her like this and told her how much she had changed.

"In what way?" she asked.

"Well, for one thing I can hear what you're saying now," I replied.

With spirit's help, she got rid of the monster and has gone back to a successful career. Oh, yes! Having assured me that she was so worthless that no man would ever look at her, she has a super boyfriend who adores her. I told her so!

When I do a reading, I have a habit of saying, "What you must do is …"

I can't count the number of times a tearful client has snuffled, "It's all very well for you to say that, but I don't think I can."

What I really should say is, "You will be helped to do so and so."

I believe that a reading does more than foretell the future. I believe that channels open up to allow spirit to come in and help, and I honestly believe that the healing and helping process continues after the reading.

I did tell you in the previous chapter that I had seen death once, but in a very positive way. A girl of about seventeen came to see me. Usually I don't like to see very young clients because they are much too vulnerable and impressionable, however, for some reason I made an exception in her case. We went through love life, family life, A-Levels, etc., but then I stopped. I peered closely at a card.

"Does your father have a friend who is dying?" I asked. "Yes, he does. An old school friend."

"Well, please tell your dad that his friend has less time than he thinks and if he wants to see him, he shouldn't put it off for too long."

A couple of months later, the father rang to thank me. He had taken my advice and gone to see his friend just after his daughter's reading. Originally his friend had been given six months to live but had deteriorated much faster than expected and had passed over not long after their meeting. The father was so grateful that he had managed to see his old friend for the last time and hadn't left it too late.

At the opposite end of the scale, a lady called Sylvie came to see me. She was a friend of a pupil of mine. She had never had a reading before and was very nervous. I put her at ease and started the reading. All of a sudden there was a power cut and we were plunged into darkness. Sylvie screamed. I found candles and lit them, but the flickering flames combined with the lashing rain and a howling gale outside did make for rather a spooky atmosphere. Sylvie's eyes were as big as saucers.

She had come to see me because she was desperate to have children and had gone through several courses of IVF without success. In fact, the doctors had more or less told her there was no hope. A feeling was definitely forming inside me.

"Sylvie," I said. "Please, please don't get too excited. I certainly don't want to give you any false hope, but I can feel a baby around you."

"You must mean an adopted baby," she said. "There is no way I can have children of my own."

"I don't know, but I can feel a baby here with us. I'm sure there is a way for you to have a child."

Sylvie went home, looking quite relieved to leave the candles and skeletal branches tapping against the windows like ghostly beings trying to gain entry. A few weeks later, my pupil said, "Guess what? A miracle's happened. Sylvie's pregnant!"

What fantastic news! I was so happy for her. She had a bouncing baby boy and, when we thought back, we realised she must have been about two days pregnant when she came to see me.

A similar thing happened with best friend Sarah. For many years she owned a beauty salon - in fact, that's how we met. I was in there being given a pedicure by Karen, one of the girls who worked for her. Karen had just got married and was telling me all about it. Sarah had a few minutes to spare and popped in for a chat. We continued talking about the wedding. Out of the blue, I said to Karen, "You're not pregnant, are you?"

"Hope not," came the reply. "I don't think so."

"Well, I can definitely feel a baby in the room."

We carried on chatting and again, unexpectedly, I asked Sarah if twins ran in her family.

"Yes, why?" she asked.

"I don't know. I just feel that one day you might have twins."

A few weeks later, it was Sarah who discovered she was pregnant, but sadly, very soon after, she suffered a miscarriage. The doctors sorted her out, but she continued to feel sick and ill. Eventually, her doctor decided she should have a D and C but luckily said he would give her a scan first. As they did the scan, there on the screen was another baby – my stunning, amazing goddaughter.

"I can't believe it," said the doctor. "You must have been expecting twins." "Probably," said Sarah. "My friend Suzi told me I was."

I was mid-way through a reading for my friend Belinda when my doorbell rang. It was a lady I had never seen before. She had got my address from a local beauty salon (not Sarah's) although how they had it, I'm not sure. The poor woman looked dreadful. "Please help me," she implored. "My husband is dying."

I didn't know what to say. I asked her in and gave her a cup of tea. As Belinda and I talked to her, it emerged that her husband had been diagnosed with bone cancer and had been given just weeks to live. It was a second marriage for both of them and they had only been together for a couple of years. They adored each other and she was distraught at the thought of losing him. I really couldn't think how I could help her, but I arranged for her to come back the next day.

Surprisingly, when I put the spread down, it looked very good. Problems around at the moment but lots of happiness in the future. Surely this couldn't be right. However, there in the immediate future was the death card. The poor woman dissolved into tears. I tried to reassure her that this meant change and new beginnings, but I don't think I convinced either of us. Nevertheless, as I concentrated on the card something changed. Death did not look sad or threatening, he looked rather jolly and happy. Now, Gran often gives me parallels with things that have happened in my own life, and as I peered at the card, my cousin Tim popped into my mind. He worked for a Health Authority and had done a Ph.D. in Bilharzia disease, a waterborne tropical illness.

"Have you been to Africa?" I asked. "Yes, earlier this year."

"Did your husband spend any time in water, not the sea but a river or a lake?" "Yes. He did a lot of windsurfing on a lake."

Things began to clear. Gran was getting quite excited.

"Please do something for me," I said. "Keep doing what the doctors tell you, but please take your husband to that hospital that specialises in tropical diseases and get him some tests. I'm not sure if it is bone cancer."

Now, I would never, never suggest that anyone ignores doctors' advice on the say so of a clairvoyant, but I didn't think it would hurt to have an extra examination.

Six months later I had a phone call. "Do you remember me? I'm the woman whose husband was dying." My heart sank. I was just about to utter words of sympathy when she carried on. "I can't speak for long. I'm at Heathrow. We're just about to fly off to Hong Kong. My stepdaughter is getting married. You were absolutely right. My husband did have a rare disease that he caught in that lake. Thanks to you it was identified and he is completely cured. I can't even begin to tell you how grateful we are to you."

My eyes filled with tears.

"Thank you Gran," I whispered. "This has been the finest thing that has happened." I felt humble, proud, grateful, and happy all at the same time. Spirit had somehow guided that lady to me and shown me how to help her. It doesn't get much better than that.

Years ago, Mrs. Butterfield had said to me, "One day, dear, with spirit's help, you will write a book."

"Don't be daft," I retorted. "I couldn't possibly write a book. English was my worst subject. Only thing I ever got a B for apart from Art."

She fixed me with her beady eye. "You mark my words, my duck. You will."

It has crossed my mind from time to time that everyone is supposed to have one book inside them, and when I went to Australia for the first time, I had the idea to write about my experiences Down Under. My friend Jane gave me a Smythson travel notebook of which I was incredibly proud, and in which I jotted down things that took my fancy during our odyssey around Australia. I even had a title for it, but somehow could never put pen to paper.

When we got back from Australia early in 2008, I was diagnosed with breast cancer. It was picked up during a routine mammogram and I am unbelievably lucky. The cancer was small, it had not spread, and was not of a particularly aggressive nature. I have nothing but praise for the expertise and kindness of the staff at Winchester and Southampton hospitals. Within a week of being recalled for another mammogram, I had been operated on and the cancer removed.

I then had to undergo five weeks of daily radiotherapy. Now, God forbid, dear reader, that you ever have to undergo this, but believe me, there is nothing to it. Okay, there are a couple of unpleasant after effects, but the actual treatment is a piece of cake. The radiographers arrange you on a bed, being very careful to get you in exactly the right position. They then leave you for a couple of minutes, during which time a machine whirrs and clicks. You cannot feel anything at all, but you do have to keep absolutely still and not twitch a whisker.

It was, however, a strange feeling knowing that I was being "nuked" and so, to take my mind off things, I used to compose the opening lines of my Australian book in my head. After a few treatments, I was lying there, listening to the machine going about its business, when a voice said quite clearly to me, "Wrong book. Write about your work and save Australia for later." And so, that was how this book came about.

I don't know why spirit chose me to use as a channel, all I know is that I have been incredibly blessed. There is a darker side to the spirit world, but the last thirty years have been a fantastic experience, and I can honestly say that I'm a very happy Medium.

Oh! Just a moment. I've got a message coming through. It's Mrs. Butterfield. Sorry, Mrs. B, what did you say?

She's chuckling. "You didn't believe me when I told you that you were going to write a book," she's saying. "But I told you so!"

THE END

BIO

Suzi Samuel opens the door to her world and invites you to experience the sweet and often funny relationship she has with her two grannies who have passed over.

With a small child and widowed after 5 years of marriage, Suzi found herself alone but rapidly aware of a whole other world. This was the start of her work as a clairvoyant and she has now been doing readings for more than thirty years with clients in many different countries.

Having negotiated the dating minefield that was the 80's and having survived quite a few, often hilarious, near brushes with matrimony, she met her gorgeous Australian, David, and, after a whirlwind courtship, married him in 1997, moving to Hampshire where they lived for several years before moving back to Australia.

Suzi now lives in New South Wales with David and her Golden Retriever, Sydney where she concentrates on writing and clairvoyant work and is very involved with the charity Legacy.

CPSIA information can be obtained at www.ICGtesting.com
Printed in the USA
BVOW02s1233110316

440001BV00001B/4/P